COMPLETE FAMILY WEALTH

COMPLETE FAMILY WEALTH

Wealth as Well-Being

Second Edition

James E. Hughes
Susan E. Massenzio
Keith Whitaker

WILEY

Published by John Wiley & Sons, Inc., Hoboken, New Jersey.
Published simultaneously in Canada.

For general information on our other products and services or for technical support, please contact our Customer Care Department within the United States at (800) 762-2974, outside the United States at (317) 572-3993 or fax (317) 572-4002.

Wiley also publishes its books in a variety of electronic formats. Some content that appears in print may not be available in electronic formats. For more information about Wiley products, visit our web site at www.wiley.com.

Library of Congress Cataloging-in-Publication Data:

ISBN: 9781119820031 (hardback),
ISBN: 9781119820048 (epub),
ISBN: 9781119820055 (ePDF)

Cover Design: Wiley
Cover Image: Wiley

SKY10031538_112221

What is very easy? To advise another.

What is very hard? To know yourself.

Thales, the first philosopher

Contents

Preface to the
Second Edition

This new edition of *Complete Family Wealth* contains a number of noteworthy changes.

We have updated the first chapter's discussion of qualitative capital to reflect the latest thinking in the field, which distinguishes among five types of non-financial wealth: human, legacy, family relationship, structural, and social. We have also included in this chapter our thoughts on ways that families can invest in this most important form of capital and measure the impact of their investment.

Upon much reflection and discussion with beneficiaries, we have included a new chapter on the subject of "The Big Reveal," the moment when recipients are supposedly introduced to their present or future financial wealth. This moment looms very large in the minds of parents, but in practice it is what happens next—the flight, fight, freeze, or flourishing—that makes all the difference. We offer recommendations on how to increase the likelihood of the lattermost of those possibilities.

Among other additions, because it comes up so often, we have included a chapter on preserving a beloved family vacation home, and we have added two appendices: one detailing a "Fiduciary Course Curriculum," for families who wish to enhance the learning (and living) of their trustees and beneficiaries, and a second that discusses "Key Practices for Families During Challenging Times," which sprang from our work with families during the pandemic but whose lessons apply to any sorts of challenges that families may face.

Finally, perhaps the biggest change to this edition is also the smallest: the inclusion of the word "well-being" on the title-page and at strategic points in the text. We have long believed in the importance of learning from the etymology of the word "wealth," which derives from "weal," with the original meaning of "well-being." Our decades of experience helping families have convinced us that perhaps the most beneficial step a family can take is to shift their understanding of wealth from finances to well-being—all else that we write about, speak about, and do stems from this reorientation in consciousness.

Preface to the First Edition

This book culls the essence of our prior books: *Family Wealth* (1997 and 2004), *Family: The Compact Among Generations* (2007), *Cycle of the Gift* (2014), *Voice of the Rising Generation* (2015), and *Family Trusts* (2016). It also captures insights that we have shared in dozens of articles, white papers, and blog posts, as well as in presentations to hundreds of audiences. We deeply appreciate all that we have learned from our many reviewers, our respondents, and the participants in these events.

Each chapter of *Complete Family Wealth* connects to others through themes and concepts; each can also be read on its own. Please feel free to pick and choose among them, based on the topics of greatest importance to you and your family.

In *Complete Family Wealth,* we have sought to present *enduring ideas* and *practices*. These are the insights and the activities that we have seen make a truly positive difference in families' lives over the long-term.

Following are some of these enduring principles, which are reflected more fully in the chapters that follow:

> *The* goal is not "beating the 'shirtsleeves to shirtsleeves' proverb" in the sense of keeping only *financial* capital in the family. Financial capital is important. But references to "the proverb" have caused many readers to think that we advocate attention to qualitative capital *for the sake of* financial capital. The opposite is the truth.

> Though our subject is "family" wealth, this wealth resides in *individual* family members. Their relationships are crucial, but the health of relationships and the family depends on the prior health of the individuals who are related.

> While "governance" (shared decision-making) is important and sometimes overlooked, too much emphasis on governance ends up imposing "forms" on the family under which it cannot "function." Sometimes it is easier for advisers to hand a family a draft constitution than to help them to live well together. But the former, if ever adopted, should serve the latter.

INTRODUCTION

An Invitation

Welcome to the journey. We hope that in reading *Complete Family Wealth* you will discover new ideas and practices that will enable your family to grow its qualitative and financial capitals long into the future.

Complete Family Wealth marks a stage in the journey of we three coauthors, at times individually, more recently together. As we invite you to join us, we begin with a short description of our paths thus far.

A Welcome from James (Jay) Hughes, Esq.

Welcome back readers of our previous books, and welcome new readers! For those of you pilgrims wearing your scallop shells and round hats and carrying your staffs, walking with us to Santiago to discover how to help your families flourish, please sit down, take off your regalia, and join Keith and Susan and me in the next steps of our common *pèlerinages*. For those of you just joining, please ask those who are already on this journey for their help and their stories of success in overcoming the obstacles their families face to flourishing.

As many readers already know, my journey to help my family deal with the proverb of "shirtsleeves to shirtsleeves in three generations" began when I was four years old. I overheard my mother, Elizabeth Buermann, in an agitated state, explaining to my father, James E. Hughes, her concerns about money and her worries about the proverb. Her worries continued until her death at the age of 95.

Why? Because her father, my grandfather, had gone bankrupt in the Depression. She had come home one day to find a "For Sale" sign on the front lawn of her home in Newark, New Jersey. Her family until then had large financial resources inherited from her grandfather, a German immigrant, an inventor, and a successful industrialist. Not knowing why that sign was there, she went into the house and found her mother. Her mother told that her father had gone bankrupt by virtue of depositing his money in his father's now busted savings and loan company. Then her mother shared with her another terrible truth. My grandmother had only a high school education, had been the single cosseted child of devoted parents, and till that day had "help" in the house. She told my mother that, as my grandfather "did not know how to work," she was going to work the next day. My grandmother worked for 50 years, into her mid-80s, as a receptionist in a hospital to provide for her family. So it is quite understandable that my mother had these fears of the proverb: she had been living it every day since her youth.

My mother's recital of these realities to my father made me want to help her put those fears aside. It also made me appreciate how emotionally pernicious the effects of the proverb are.

As readers of *Family Wealth* know, I met the proverb again many years later, in 1974, when I was asked by the sons of an enormously successful businessman in Singapore to come visit their father.

I was naturally curious why I, a still very wet-behind-the-ears private-client attorney, was being invited to travel halfway round the world at substantial cost to the family when there must be excellent legal counsel available in Singapore. When the day of the meeting came, I still had no idea why I had been invited. After entering his office and solving, over tea, all the macroeconomic problems of the world, I was still wondering. Finally, this worldly-wise man said, "Mr. Hughes, you are probably wondering why I invited you here. We Chinese have a proverb, 'Rice paddy to rice paddy in three generations.' I don't want that to happen to my family. Can you help us using the techniques of families in America to solve this problem?" I was happy to discover that I could help him.

In the years since 1974, as I have traveled to meet with families around the world, I have heard the same idea expressed in varying ways. The shirt-sleeves proverb turns out to be culturally universal, capturing a great truth about wealth and human behavior.

As a result, the proverb has been the question that has dominated my personal and professional life.

One of the most wonderfully positive parts of my journey has been to be a part of my parents' creation of a flourishing family from the ashes of both of theirs. Today we are a family, including in my case, wonderful additions from my wife Jackie's family. We are a flourishing, tightly knit group of three living generations with a strong bond to the gifts of my parents' generation. Our tribe meets my test of a flourishing family: every generation has the contact information of their first cousins and, if they called any one of them, their voices would be immediately recognized. Do we face obstacles to continuing this flourishing? Yes, we do. Are we facing them head on? Yes, we are.

To face the proverb's challenges, I set out to meet, learn from, and befriend remarkable professionals who share my passion to serve families. These friends and colleagues are too many to name here. Two of them, Susan and Keith, joined me in this effort to produce *Complete Family Wealth*, and with them I wrote two other books, *The Cycle of the Gift* (2013) and *Voice of the Rising Generation* (2014). We came together, over 10 years ago, at a time when I had started to doubt whether I had anything more to say. Our conversations opened new vistas to me of ideas and of hope. I came to see myself in the true elder role: not leading or doing but rather convening those who wish to learn and encouraging those who seek to act.

I am now in my 75th year of life and 50th year of practice. I am deeply humbled to see that, over the past 20 years, our little books have taken on lives of their own. They have done so—and I hope that *Complete Family Wealth* will do so—because you, the reader, will, I believe, find at least one suggestion here that will prompt you to have the courage to believe that the shirt sleeve proverb can be avoided. I believe it can!

A Welcome from Dr. Susan Massenzio

I was born into a family of second-generation immigrants to America. Resilience, hard work, and community were values that were woven into the fabric of my family as well as the families of many other immigrants.

I was fortunate to have loving grandparents and parents who led their lives with integrity and generosity. I learned at a very young age that money was a means to independence, choice, and the ability to be generous with people whom one loves. I was also gifted with good health, a good mind, and an adaptive attitude. I inherited much qualitative wealth.

My grandfather was very resourceful and made several good real estate investments, which he left equally to his four children. My father started a family business with his brother that had its share of success and hard times. I witnessed firsthand the realities of a family business: the challenge of succession without adequate planning, the conflicts that ensued, and the impact on the business created by spouses who married into the family.

My mother was a remarkable woman—she lived to be 101 years old—who decided to take on a second job as the family business was failing, to provide extra money to send me to college. Upon graduation, I worked in a state institution for children with special needs and then I transitioned to teaching special needs children in a public school. It was during my time teaching children with special needs who were living with their families that I saw the impact of having a child with special needs on the family. This experience prompted me to go on to graduate school with a focus on family dynamics.

For several years, I taught undergraduate and graduate courses in organizational psychology with a focus on the application of psychology to organizations and families. For most of my career, I have focused on the application of psychological theories and practices to positively impact leadership development in public and private companies, foundations, and families.

I believe that my professional journey has come full circle. It has gone from personal involvement with family business, to professional work with families with children with special needs, to corporate leadership, and then to families with the special need of wealth, to benefit family members and the communities of which they are a part.

What money I have, I have earned. I know the pride that comes from earning one's own money and the joy of being able to use it to help others. I have also been fortunate to have enjoyed the peace that comes from the sense of having enough.

In recent years, I have had the good fortune to work with two wonderful professionals: my loving partner, Keith Whitaker, and our dear friend, Jay Hughes. I have also been able to experience the joys and challenges of great corporate leaders and enterprising families with significant wealth. My hope is that I will be able to continue to have a positive impact on the lives of others through my own life experience, education, and commitment to cultivating qualitative wealth.

A Welcome from Dr. Keith Whitaker

My journey into this field began with my 17th birthday. I grew up in a middle-class home. I didn't think much about money; we didn't have too much or too little. Then, the afternoon of my birthday, my mother took me aside and said, "I want you to know that your grandfather has been very successful in business, so you can do whatever you like in your life."

I remember feeling at the time that this was an odd comment. I already believed I could do whatever I liked, with or without money.

However, learning about my grandfather's financial success did make me feel different than I had before. I felt that more was expected of me. "To whom much is given much shall be required." When I went off to college—which my grandfather paid for—I made a point of bringing him my transcript each semester, to show what I had achieved. With the gift, I felt a responsibility.

I also felt free—free to pursue a subject that truly interested me, classical philosophy, without focusing on my expected salary. I didn't have any student loans. I pursued a teaching career without the fear of being destitute.

These are some of the positive elements of the experience of learning about family wealth at an early age. But I found that there are also negatives.

For example, the flip side of freedom is a sort of lightness. This is a sense that no matter what I did, I could make up for bad choices or not deal with the frustrations that most other people face. For example, I loved philosophy but not the many tiresome parts of the job of teaching, and so I left it. Since that time, I do have some regrets, which money can't eliminate.

The flip side of feeling special is that you can become a mark. People with money often fall in with others who seek them out for their money. I was taken advantage of at times, and it was deeply hurtful.

The flip side of feeling gifted is entanglement. As a recipient, I felt I should give a return to my family by taking on various responsibilities around wealth management, trusteeship, service on the foundation board, and so on. These responsibilities took up a lot of time, taking me away from sorting out my own dreams. While I learned much from this work, it was not my true calling. It took a long time for me truly to become my own person.

When Jay invited me to join him in this journey, I knew that we would make excellent partners. We share the classic understanding of financial capital as a tool to pursue the ultimate qualitative goal: the inquiry into and the practice of living well.

The same is the case with Susan, whom I invited to join me in the journey of work and life over a decade ago. Little did I know then that I would learn from her that our true resources are our hearts and minds, and that our greatest gift is time, used well.

The Path Ahead

To orient you in this journey, we have organized the book into four main parts:

> Part One (Chapters 1, 2, and 3) lays out the subject matter under discussion, the "what." They address what we mean by family, wealth, and enterprise.
>
> Part Two (Chapters 4 through 11) discusses the host of roles crucial to family enterprise flourishing. The "who" includes the rising generation, parents, grandparents, spouses, elders, trustees, and beneficiaries, advisers, and friends.
>
> Part Three (Chapters 12 through 23) moves to the "how," specific practices that families can use to grow their complete family wealth.

We end with a conclusion on individual flourishing that aims to give you best wishes and thoughtful guidance as you continue your own journey and, finally, with an epilogue that seeks to peer a little way into the future.

For this second edition, we have also added two appendices: the first, a curriculum for teaching family members about trusts; and the second, a review of practices that can help your family navigate difficult times, such as the COVID pandemic.

Again, feel free to read these chapters in order or pick and choose based on your interests. Each one stands on its own.

PART ONE

CHAPTER 1

Complete Wealth

In the late 20th century, when *Family Wealth* was published, its subtitle was *Keeping It in the Family*.

Many readers assumed that the "it" referred to money. After all, doesn't the proverb—"shirtsleeves to shirtsleeves in three generations"—refer to a family's economic condition?

From this assumption, an entire industry has grown, an industry aimed at helping families correct their family dynamics to preserve and grow their financial capital.

Likewise, many readers, family leaders, and advisers have concluded that the most important thing is to seek to beat the proverb and do what it takes to keep their financial capital in the family.

Right Understanding

But this conclusion is wrong.

The "it" is not money. It is the family's well-being. That is its true wealth. We encompass this well-being by speaking about "qualitative wealth"—the family's human, legacy, family relationship, structural, and social capital. This wealth as well-being is the goal, which the family's quantitative wealth, its financial capital, rightly serves.

Beating the proverb is not a matter of simply using various tools and techniques—family meetings, values clarification, communication ground rules, and so on and so forth—to make family members better stewards of their money. Keeping your money in your family is not necessarily a bad thing. But it is not the main thing. It is only one-fifth of the task. And it is the least important fifth, when it comes to happiness.

The goal of *Complete Family Wealth* is to help you identify, inventory, and grow your true, or complete, wealth as a family. This complete wealth far transcends money. Growing complete wealth also meets the criticisms of those—from Andrew Carnegie to proponents of social justice—who denounce inherited financial capital as bad for families and for society. Complete family wealth improves the lives of family members and benefits the communities of which they are a part.

One family leader captured the distinction for us by quoting her grand-mother. This wise woman, she said, would often say, "Our family has always been rich, and we've sometimes had money." There is the distinction between qualitative and quantitative capital in a nutshell.

As with any important undertaking, it is crucial to begin with right understanding. To that end, as you read this book and think about wealth, notice when you automatically identify that term with financial capital. That is the identification we are seeking to challenge and to substitute with wealth as well-being. If you choose to pursue the journey of family wealth, be clear just what kinds of wealth you are trying to keep in the family.

Complete Wealth

We have said that complete family wealth comprises five aspects of qualitative capital—human, legacy, family relationship, structural, and social—and the family's quantitative assets, its financial capital. The goals of the rest of this chapter are to define these forms of capital, outline ways of growing them, and suggest a method for measuring the growth of qualitative capital.

Rarely do families measure their qualitative capital. That's because they often do not even recognize that they own this type of capital. But can you imagine any enterprise being successful if it didn't track most of its capital?

The failure to acknowledge, measure, and grow the qualitative capital of a family is the principal cause for the failure of family flourishing.

In contrast, investing in the family's qualitative capital—investing time, energy, and financial wealth—is perhaps the greatest "impact investment" a family can make.

As you read, you will likely notice overlaps among the five aspects of qualitative capital. That is because each one captures an aspect of the same thing: the family's true flourishing.

The Five Types of Qualitative Capital

Human Capital

The Human Capital of a family consists of the individuals who make up the family. Their human capital includes their physical and emotional well-being as well as each member's ability to find meaningful work, establish a positive sense of identity, and pursue his or her own happiness.

FIGURE 1.1 The Qualitative Capital Wheel.

HUMAN CAPITAL
Individual family
members' physical
and emotional health
and resilience

LEGACY CAPITAL
The family's core
values and purpose –
the "Family Brand"

Qualitative
Capital

SOCIAL CAPITAL
Commitment to
communities
beyond the family

FAMILY
RELATIONSHIP
CAPITAL
Family's members
ability to build strong
interpersonal
connections
within the family

STRUCTURAL
CAPITAL
Governance structures,
policies, and practices
that promote effective
decision-making

Legacy Capital

Legacy capital consists of the family's core values and sense of shared purpose. In many ways, it can be considered the "Family Brand"—what makes the family distinct and gives the family members a sense of shared identity.

Family Relationship Capital

Effective communication is at the heart of every successful family. A family's ability to engage and support communication across generations is particularly important. This ability to build strong interpersonal connections within the family is family relationship capital.

Structural Capital

Families with significant wealth or businesses often operate within a network of trusts, partnerships, contracts, and other legal or business relationships. Structural capital consists of an understanding of this network and the ability to navigate it effectively.

Social Capital

Families shape and are shaped by the communities of which they are a part. Commitment to these communities gives families a strength that comes from serving something greater than themselves. This commitment to communities *beyond* the family is social capital.

Financial Capital

The financial capital of a family is the property it owns. This property may include cash, public securities, privately held company stock, and interests in private partnerships.

    The focus of this book is qualitative capital, not financial capital. But that doesn't mean that we think that financial capital is unimportant. Financial capital greatly contributes to families' ability to cultivate their other forms of capital. It makes possible quality health care, education, philanthropy, and the time and opportunities to come together and talk about building and sustaining a shared dream. The opportunity to cultivate these qualitative assets is a great gift, which financial capital makes possible.

Growing Capital

Wealth preservation is a dynamic, not a static, process. To succeed, each generation of the family must adopt a first-generation—a wealth-creating generation—mindset.

Any family whose complete wealth—qualitative and quantitative—is simply maintaining value rather than growing it is either in or in danger of entering into a state of decay or entropy. A family, like every investor, must maximize its return on capital if it is to achieve the growth necessary for preservation over a long period of time. What are some of the things a family can do to grow its various forms of qualitative capital?

Human Capital

With respect to its human capital, a family can consider implementing the following practices:

1. Promote each member's individual flourishing. (For more on the psychological aspects of individual flourishing, see the Conclusion.) This includes providing the best possible medical care to every family member whose pursuit of happiness is blocked by addiction or physical or mental illness.
2. Ensure that every family member's basic requirements for food, shelter, and clothing are met, and for members who experience a life emergency, that those needs are met at a level adequate to allow them to regain the capacity for the pursuit of individual happiness.
3. Emphasize the importance of work to an individual's sense of self-worth and assist each family member in finding the work that most enhances that individual's pursuit of happiness. All such work is of equal value to the growth of the family's human capital, regardless of its financial reward.
4. Encourage all family members, especially rising generation members, to develop a strong sense of personal identity separate from the family's financial success.
5. Promote the family's geographic diversification. The world is becoming smaller every day. Families must participate in all corners of the world if they are to meet today's global challenges.

Legacy Capital

With regard to legacy capital:

1. Help each member of the family clarify his or her values. Discuss what matters most to each of you. Identify areas of overlap, of shared family values, and respect areas of difference.
2. Share stories of the family's history, and of the history of the various families that preceded yours. Tell stories of failure and disappointment as well as of success. Sometimes the stories of failure followed by striving and achievement are the most powerful ones.
3. Honor family traditions, whether around holidays, birthdays, anniversaries, or other important milestones in the lives of family members and of the family as a whole. Discuss which traditions family members are eager to preserve and celebrate, and which some or all family members might be ready to let go of.

Family Relationship Capital

Here are some ways for a family to grow its family relationship capital:

1. Consider beginning or continuing the practice of holding regular, well-designed and facilitated family meetings to discuss topics of importance to the family as a whole.
2. Set aside time during a family meeting to work on enhancing effective communication among family members. That may take the form of learning about individuals' particular communication styles, understanding how different styles complement or clash, and developing strategies for navigating points of friction.
3. Talk about the reasons for including family members' spouses in important family discussions. What are the fears of or challenges to doing so? What do family members see as the benefits? Spouses often bring valuable perspectives to family discussions, in addition to being the parents of the future rising generation.
4. If the family suffers from breakdowns of trust, respect, or fairness among family members, use resources to secure consultation for members to surface, manage, and possibly resolve these conflicts.

Structural Capital

When it comes to growing structural capital, families can:

1. Rapidly provide clear information on all family governance matters to all family members at the highest level of each person's ability to understand and seek feedback.
2. Invite trust counsel or other advisers to design engaging educational sessions to inform family members about their wealth structures, their functions and goals, and the roles and responsibilities attendant on these structures.
3. Develop a leadership development plan that takes into account the future needs of the family, the evolution of its wealth or business structures, the true interest of family members in serving in leadership positions, and the needs they have to develop the skills and knowledge to serve effectively.

Social Capital

Many of the practices in the rest of this book describe how families can grow their social capital. Some steps families may particularly wish to consider include:

1. Talk about ways that all family members, regardless of age or stage of development, give back to others and find joy in giving.
2. Consider building or amending philanthropic structures to give individual family members' choices in how they deploy charitable resources.
3. Provide rising generation family members with opportunities to connect with the larger community through service in the family's business efforts or in its philanthropies.
4. Consider ending every family gathering with a brief gratitude exercise, in which members envision someone in the family they wish to thank and identify ways to offer those thanks.

Financial Capital

We will leave the growth of a family's financial capital to the many other authors who have made this capital their focus.[1]

---

[1] We share additional thoughts on the relation between financial capital and the qualitative capitals in Chapter 21, "Financial Capital." There we also summarize two practices related to the intersection of the qualitative and quantitative capitals, Investor Allocation and the Family Bank.

We add only these two considerations, reflective of the often-difficult relationship that families have with their financial capital.

First, many family members who have inherited financial capital do not know how difficult it is to create it. They may feel awed by the presence of the wealth creator and define success as the creation of great financial capital. Defining success in financial terms can create a sense of not being good enough. In addition, their experience of the wealth creator may have some negative associations. As a result, later-generation family members often do not feel the same motivations that fueled the creativity of the originator of the family's financial capital. This is a problem for the family's financial sustainability. The problem is compounded if the family imagines or, worse, assumes that every member will turn out to be an entrepreneur. Such assumptions can become counterproductive. Only through undertaking the hard work of identifying and supporting each family member's own talents and dreams can the family hope to see—perhaps—the blossoming of the entrepreneurial spirit that will, in turn, contribute to the larger family's financial capital.

Second, most families have a hard time talking about financial capital. Money is perhaps the last and most pervasive taboo. Many times, this is for bad reasons: family members feel uneducated, disempowered, and embarrassed. This silence comes with a real opportunity cost. As we will discuss more fully in Chapters 14 and 17, long-term success depends on helping family members talk productively about money with each other.

That said, as with any taboo, there are also some good reasons that people are hesitant to talk about money. No one knows better than people with significant financial capital that many others (including even family members at times) can end up seeing you only for your money. Not talking about money can be a sound defensive measure. The chapters that follow aim to help readers develop safe ways to talk about financial capital, ways that preserve and promote the family's four qualitative capitals.

A Provocative Comparison

Before turning to the question of measuring the various types of qualitative capital, consider briefly a quantitative comparison. Tally up a rough estimate of how much your family spends each year to account for, preserve, and manage its financial capital. That spending may include asset management fees, advisory fees, legal fees, accounting fees, custody fees, and many others.

Next, think about the types of qualitative capital and the activities we described to grow them. How much does your family invest in them? Probably quite a bit when it comes to sending young adults to college or paying for major medical care. But what about on an ongoing basis? What about investing in the proactive growth of qualitative capital?

(Notice the difference here, familiar to any business owner, between operating expenses—such as those related to managing assets—and investment, which is an expenditure meant to grow your assets.)

You likely have a budget that covers the costs of managing your financial capital. Have you ever considered an investment plan for growing your qualitative capital? If you had such an investment plan, how would it compare to the budget for your financial capital? What would that comparison say about the relative importance of the different forms of capital in your family's life?

Measuring Qualitative Capital

Many families keep track of their financial capital on an annual or even quarterly or monthly basis. Careful stewarding of balance sheets and income statements is critical to the management of the family's financial capital.

Unfortunately, these efforts often don't extend to the family's qualitative capital. Without an assessment of qualitative capital, the family and individual balance sheets are incomplete and will not measure the extent to which a family is growing its complete wealth.

One way to measure, manage, and grow qualitative capital is Family Qualitative Capital Management, a program we developed at Wise Counsel Research. In this section we share a brief description of this process.

First, every twelve months, we measure our client families' qualitative capital. To do so, we designed a tool we call the Family Balance Sheet. It takes each family member about 20–30 minutes to fill it out online. The Family Balance Sheet produces topline results for the family that show its scores in human, legacy, family relationship, structural, and social capital.

Second, we aggregate all family members' responses to create a Family Qualitative Capital Report. This Report identifies the family's areas of strength and weakness in the five forms of qualitative capital. Based on the family's results, we include in the Report relevant and actionable recommendations for each family member and for the family as a whole.

Third, we meet with the family to review the Family Qualitative Capital Report. (Each individual family member's report is confidential to him or her, but everyone sees the Family Report.) The most important part of this annual meeting is to help the family discuss and decide on a Qualitative Action Plan. This Plan may include specific objectives such as enhancing cross-generational communication, engaging and educating rising generation family members, and creating effective governance structures. The Family Qualitative Capital Action Plan ensures that the family always proceeds forward in a thoughtful, deliberate manner, that responds to its true needs, and makes the most of family members' engagement and the resources committed to these efforts.

Fourth, family members pursue their agreed-upon Qualitative Action Plan in concert with appropriate specialists. These may include family office staff, attorneys, individual or family counselors, or governance specialists. This is the same as what is called "manager selection" in the world of quantitative capital. You don't expect one person to manage all your different financial assets. So why expect one consultant or adviser to help you with your different forms of qualitative capital?

Fifth, after six months, we reconvene a family meeting to evaluate progress toward the agreed-upon objectives and make any needed adjustments to the Qualitative Capital Action Plan.

Sixth, in the final month of each annual engagement, we meet once more with family leadership to summarize progress, identify changes in the family system, update the Family Qualitative Action Plan, and discuss overarching goals for the next year of the family's work together.

No doubt you've noticed the parallel between the process of Family Qualitative Capital Management and the process of financial wealth management.

There's one crucial way in which the two differ. As fascinating and as important as it is, financial wealth management is not an end in itself. Financial capital is a means to pursue other ends, such as security, comfort, health, meaningful experiences, etc.

In contrast, qualitative capital is both a means and an end. Having strong qualitative capital allows your family members to do more—to work together effectively, to make good decisions, to sustain their family business or family finances over generations. But it also allows them to be more—to be healthier and happier in their individual lives and with each other. It promotes true "wealth as well-being."

CHAPTER 2

Family Enterprise

Affinity

In this chapter, we will share insights on family flourishing and family enterprise. But first what do we mean by family? This is not as simple a question as may seem at first.

One of the principles that we have seen prove itself time and again in our work is that the families who flourish over time understand themselves as families of affinity.[1] A family of affinity does not limit its sense of identity to blood or genetic lineage. It sees itself as linked by a common mission and a sense of "differentness." It recognizes the paradox that acting altruistically—for the sake of others' good—is key to the family's own well-being. Families of affinity add members through marriage and partnership; spiritual relationships (such as godparents); mentorship; friendship; and shared service, as in business or philanthropy. Families of affinity also include trusted advisers who have come to know the family members through years of service and who have proven that they seek the family's best interest.

How can you encourage your family to think in terms of affinity rather than blood? To take some small but powerful examples, when the families of affinity that we know have a family meeting, they often put the last names of both parents—patriarch and matriarch—atop the agenda. And they spend

---

[1] For a deeper exploration of the concept of families of affinity, see Jay Hughes, *Family: The Compact among Generations* (New York: Bloomberg, 2007), Introduction and Chapter 1.

time honoring the stories of other "married-ins," to remind everyone that the family tree has many roots. Such actions affirm that the family's first principle is inclusion.

A family of affinity rarely arises on its own. Usually it takes years or even generations to cultivate. That cultivation begins with being clear about the goal. As you begin this journey, ask yourself:

- Who in my family shares this vision of family based on affinity rather than blood?
- Who are the members of my family of affinity?
- Who could be potential members of my family of affinity?

Flourishing

"Flourishing" is a term that has been much in common parlance over the last decade or two, as it captures a sense of happiness as an activity, not a static state of contentment or satisfaction. We use it interchangeably with well-being to indicate the full range of true wealth for human beings.

We have had the good fortune to work with many flourishing families over the past 50 years. We have also had the great privilege to interview families around the globe for our research. This research, known as the 100-Year Families Study, focuses on families who have successfully transitioned a major family enterprise through at least two generations. They measure their achievements in decades, even centuries. We have sought their insights into what has worked: What factors have allowed them to flourish together for so long?[2]

From these conversations and our observations, we have distilled the following key elements in family flourishing. This is not an exhaustive list. It provides a beginning to thought and action.

Keys to Family Flourishing

First, at some point in their early history, flourishing families form the intention to build not only a great fortune but also a great family. This is the fundamental intention, without which little else can follow.

---

[2] For an overview of the 100-Year Families Study, see Dennis Jaffe et al., *Good Fortune* (Boston: Wise Counsel Research, 2014).

Second, these families articulate and share their core values, and they keep those values alive through example, education, and further discussions.

Third, these families respect and encourage individual differences. They support members' separation and individuation as members of the family discover their own dreams.

Fourth, these families keep their collective focus on their strengths. They face challenges squarely but don't let liabilities become their focus.

Fifth, flourishing families share history with family stories that are told and retold through the generations. They sustain and celebrate their traditions and rituals.

Sixth, parents see themselves as both teachers and learners.

Seventh, such families understand the importance of individual stages of development and integrate that understanding into parenting.

Keys for Family Flourishing Amid Wealth

In addition to these fundamental keys to flourishing, our research and experience have identified four other factors specific to flourishing within the context of financial capital.

First, giving wisely: doing so requires thought and care on the part of both givers and recipients.

Second, flourishing families encourage and promote individual identities separate from financial wealth. This task is especially important for the family's rising generation.

Third, such families use trusts, and they make sure that these trusts are primarily human rather than merely legal relationships.

Fourth, philanthropy provides these families a shared focus.

These keys to family flourishing share important characteristics. They reflect that families are made up of individuals. For the family to flourish, its individual members must flourish. They also reflect that every family has its own culture, shaped by its history, its stories, its founding values, and the values and dreams of its present members. No one individual's plans for the family, no matter how grand, will succeed if those plans run against the family's shared culture. Finally, every family belongs to a larger society that shapes its members and their choices. No family can chart its path as a family without considering the impact that the larger society will have on it and its members.

Based on these observations, we suggest reflecting on these three questions regarding your own family:

1. Is each individual member flourishing?
2. Does your family enjoy a *shared* culture aimed at promoting the *individual* flourishing of its members?
3. Do family members know *how* to chart their own paths apart from the family enterprise?

The Three-Circle Model

So far, we have discussed wealth and family. When a family has the intention to work together over generations to grow all its forms of capital, it creates a combination that we call *family enterprise*.

Enterprise is a business term. But families do not have to own and manage a business to be enterprising. Many of the enterprising families we know sold their operating businesses years or generations ago.

The first key to leading a family enterprise well is to recognize that it is composed of different parts that, as closely connected as they are, have different goals and different ways of operating.

The three main parts of any family enterprise are family, owners, and management. Family is the family of affinity. Owners include all those who own title to family capital, whether they are individuals, boards of directors, or trustees and beneficiaries of family trusts. Management can include the managers of a family-owned or controlled business, financial managers of family assets, and the advisers to the managers, owners, and family members (such as attorneys and accountants).

These parts—family, owners, and management—are at the heart of one of the most helpful models for family enterprise ever developed: the "Three-Circle Model" developed originally by Renato Tagiuri and John Davis of Harvard University (see Figure 2.1).

The Three-Circle Model is helpful in many ways.

First, it underscores that while the three circles of family enterprise form one system, each circle has its own priority. For family, that is *inclusion*. For ownership, it is *preservation* (e.g., minimizing income or transfer taxes or shielding assets from potential creditors). For management, it is *performance*.

FIGURE 2.1 The Three-Circle Model.

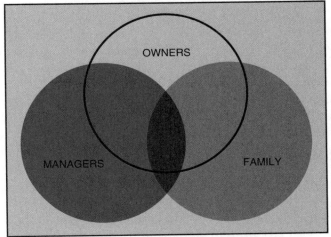

Source: Based on John Davis and Renato Tagiuri, 1996.

Troubles arise when the priority from one circle dominates the others. For example, the desire to preserve assets may keep ownership very limited, such as by excluding spouses. Likewise, management may want to improve performance by keeping "unprofessional" family members and owners at arm's length. And ownership and management may conflict over the amount of risk to take on in the pursuit of outsized returns.

Second, the model helps family enterprises locate the proper points at which to understand and resolve common conflicts. Some of the most common conflicts and challenges that arise in family enterprises include:

- Parent-child and sibling conflict over managerial control.
- Conflicts over managerial strategy and direction.
- Conflicts over ownership strategy (e.g., keep vs. sell).
- Conflicts between shareholders who are also managers versus shareholders who are outside the business, for example, over whether to reinvest profits or distribute them as dividends.
- Conflicts over employment and compensation of family members.
- Tensions between the spouses of family members who are owners or managers in the business.
- Failure of communication and understanding between trustees (family or nonfamily), the legal owners of title, and beneficiaries—especially when,

by the third generation, most, if not all, of the family's financial capital may be held in trust.

Most of these conflicts arise when people do not acknowledge the overlaps among the three circles. The starting point for resolving these conflicts is to acknowledge the different factors in them: the family needs, the needs of management, and the needs and responsibilities of owners.

Another helpful feature of the Three-Circle Model is that it gives enterprising families a way to visualize and understand where they are putting most of their efforts—and what areas they may be ignoring.

Imagine that the size of each circle represents the amount of time and care that your family enterprise devotes to family, ownership, and management. Which circles get bigger and which get smaller?

For example, is the management of an operating business or the management of the family's financial capital what occupies the most time and attention? If so, then your diagram may look more like Figure 2.2.

Or does your family enterprise focus most on who owns which shares and who elects directors? Do you spend most of your time and care on estate planning and its various structures? If so, then perhaps your diagram looks like Figure 2.3.

FIGURE 2.2 The reality for many family enterprises.

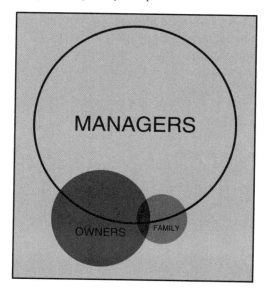

FIGURE 2.3 When ownership is the priority.

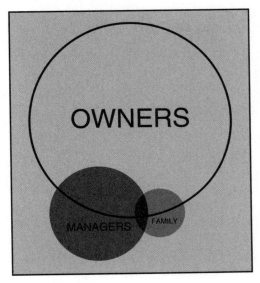

These two variations on the Three-Circle Model are the most common. It is not at all rare for either the management circle or the ownership circle to dwarf the other two. In both cases, the family circle gets smaller and smaller. If that is the case in your family, then your task is evident: to try to do what you can to grow that family circle. Ideally, for long-term success, the family circle should be larger than the other two, not smaller (see Figure 2.4).

By growing the family circle, you ensure that your family members have ways of connecting and spending time together apart from business or wealth management. You will also lay the foundation for communicating appropriate information about the financial capital broadly throughout the family, so that even those who are not in management know how it is doing. By growing the family circle, you can create a sense of identity that honors the important place of the financial capital without minimizing or excluding members who are not active within management.

Active Ownership

In addition to keeping the family circle strong, family enterprises need to pay serious attention to the ownership circle. Not doing so is often a crucial

FIGURE 2.4 Giving family its place.

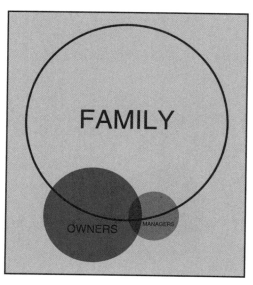

failing. Part of the problem is that most people think of ownership as a legal matter. It is. But it is even more a moral matter. The ownership circle is about *taking ownership* in the sense of taking responsibility, for yourself, your family, and its impact on the world.

Family owners are usually unaware of their responsibilities as owners, unsure about the relationships among their ownership interests, and, indeed, unclear about what they own. As a result, family members tend to be passive owners: they defer on strategic questions to management.

The clearest sign of this challenge is when many family members feel that questions of ownership are taboo or out of bounds.

Families cultivate *active* owners by making sure that all family member owners understand that:

- Ownership is a responsibility; management is a calling.
- That said, the enterprise is not "they" or "them" versus the family as "we" or "us."
- Passive ownership leads to paternalism: "Let us take care of you"—as well as resentment: "You should have known better!" Neither bodes well for long-term flourishing.

- Managing risk is a complex discipline that every owner must undertake, and the balance between taking too much risk and taking too little risk is one that can be learned and managed. (This point is especially important for family members who are not in business or not investment professionals. Such members often overestimate risk out of the fear of making mistakes.)
- Trustees, by their duty of prudence, are entropic owners because they cannot take the same risks as the stakeholder owners of other competing enterprises.
- Beneficiaries must step up to be active stakeholder owners. Doing so requires meeting regularly with trustees and asking questions in the effort to learn.
- Family owners must possess a basic understanding of systems theory, leadership science, the process of leadership transitions, and methods for assessing the health of the enterprise and the performance of management.
- Family owners must communicate with each other and truly listen to each other, to develop their dreams for the enterprise as it evolves beyond the dream of the founder or creator generation.
- Family owners must affirm, honor, and express gratitude to their managers, family, and nonfamily. Doing so energizes the system and keeps it vital.
- To pursue these activities, it is wise for family owners to hold an owners meeting at least annually. This meeting could also serve as an opportunity to do a check-up on family members' own estate plans, insurance needs, and related financial matters. Management can plan the meeting and curate content, based on appropriate back-and-forth beforehand with family members. Such a meeting may be a good occasion to invite in the family's various advisers to make sure owners have a strong connection with them and know who to call with questions or to learn more.
- Family owners should also use the family's resources to attend educational sessions where they can learn how to increase their five forms of qualitative capital.
- Young family members learn best by spending time in the family enterprise's operations, whether that is a shop floor, a trading desk, or an office, to experience the family's work and to see the impact that it has on others' lives, too.
- A family enterprise faces just a few, critical transitions to manage in each generation, and no short-term transactions are likely to make a comparable difference in the enterprise's success or failure.

- Family owners' prime responsibility is to keep their focus, with a beginner's mind, on the strategic level and not succumb to tactical thinking appropriate to short-term problems. The strategic question is not just how to *preserve* the family's complete wealth but rather how to *grow* it.

If shared intention or a shared dream provides the overall motivation for the journey of family wealth, then educated, active ownership is the means for pursuing that journey.

Transition

Since family enterprises are always growing and changing, perhaps the most crucial challenge facing them is transition.

Within a family enterprise, transition can involve at least four possibly parallel sets of changes:

1. Family transition—the transition from one generation to the next, bringing with it new roles for family members and new methods of communication.
2. Ownership transition—the transition of ownership within the family (and sometimes to nonfamily member directors or trustees), which brings with it questions of how to do so efficiently and effectively; this transition often involves the problem of how to foster active ownership when most, if not all, of the family's financial capital is held in trust. In most families, 90 percent or more of the financial capital is held in trust by the third generation. This "trust wave" can help preserve financial capital, but it can be deadening to the family's qualitative capital.[3]
3. Board transition—if the family has a business board or a Family Council (as described in Chapter 20), this transition can impact the enterprise's strategic direction.

---

[3] For more on the positive and negative long-term effects of trust, see George Marcus, with Peter Dobkin Hall, *Lives in Trust* (Boulder, CO: Westview Press, 1992). List adapted from Doud, *Challenges and Opportunities in Family Business Succession*, 59 NYU Institute on Federal Taxation 1401, no. 2 (2001).

4. Management transition—this transition raises questions about the overall direction of the business or investment policy along with questions about selecting and evaluating appropriate managers.

Each of these transitions is crucial, and often several of them take place at the same time.

An added complication is that family enterprises require different types of leaders at different points in their development and transition. For example, the most famous leaders in business management are often "leaders in front." Such leadership can be crucial in a crisis or in a new venture. Leaders in front have passion, vision, creativity, and a sense of their own calling as an inspiration to others.

The problem for family enterprises is that their long-term task is to enhance the flourishing of all members. In such cases, more effective leaders might be "leaders from behind," who help all of the members of the enterprise find their own paths. While a leader in front may be essential to the creation of a family's financial capital or its preservation in a crisis, too much leading in front will retard the development of other family members and so eventually sap the family's qualitative capital.

Finally, family enterprises need to be aware of the different uses of transactional and transformational leadership. Transactional leaders meet and overcome today's issues while transformational leaders meet and overcome the issues of the future. The former helps a family enterprise meet and eat for a day; the latter not only helps a family eat for its current lifetime but also plans for the enterprise to provide food for generations to come.

Navigating these different transitions and styles requires great care, patience, and communication. Again, the remaining chapters in this book and the tools they contain are designed to help you prepare for and manage this task of navigation. At this point, ask yourself these questions to orient yourself to what lies ahead:

- In your family enterprise, which of the circles gets the most attention: management, ownership, or family? Which gets the least?
- Which type of leadership—if any—prevails in your family enterprise now? Which seems most needed?
- Where is your family enterprise in the journey of educating *active owners*?

Time

One of the great virtues of family enterprises is that their lives far exceed the lifespans of individuals. And yet, when it comes to thinking about complete family wealth, people often fail to apply the appropriate time frames. The focus is too short-term and individual, and family goals for achievement are set far too low.

Time should be measured by the generation. Otherwise, how can a family address whether it will still be together in the fourth generation? Short-term for a family is 20 years, intermediate-term is 50 years, and long-term is 100 years or more.

Most of us know that abandoning a process too soon, because it seems too hard, is the most common reason that endeavors fail. Families who choose to start the journey of long-term wealth growth—and the growth of their complete wealth—face the daunting fact that, if they are successful, this process will never end. They must decide to continue the process literally for all the generations to come.

To help you decide whether to begin this process, we offer our favorite metaphor for growing family wealth: the copper beech tree. If you don't know what a copper beech tree looks like and you want to see one, go to Rhode Island and look in the front yards of many Newport mansions. When fully mature, a copper beech tree is one of the largest trees in the northeastern forest. It may take five or six adults, or 10 children, holding hands to ring its trunk. Once mature, a copper beech tree will live for centuries.

Why is this beautiful tree our favorite metaphor for successful long-term wealth preservation by a family? Because it takes courage to plant a tree that takes 150 years to mature. No one who does so will ever see it full grown. And it takes good fortune for it to mature. Think of the hurricanes, ice and snow, pests, and fire that may consume the tree while it is too young to withstand those hazards. Further, it takes care. It must contend with humans who want to cut it down for its wood, and with governments that want to put a road or a new housing development where it stands. Families, too, need courage, care, and good luck.

We'll close here with a story told in *Family Wealth* about a copper beech tree. In the nineteenth century, Marshal Lyautey, one of Napoleon III's generals, was reported to have the most beautiful garden in France. Standing with his head gardener, looking out over his estate, he observed the wonderful specimens of the world's great trees planted there. Lyautey then turned to the gardener and said, "I see no copper beech tree." His gardener replied,

"But, *mon général,* such a tree takes 150 years to grow." Lyautey, without a second's hesitation, said, "Then we must plant today—we have no time to waste."

Like the planting of a copper beech tree, to embark on the journey of complete family wealth is an extraordinary act: the members who initiate the process will never know whether they were ultimately successful. If you are courageous and you want to be a wealth creator in the most profound sense, get started. There is no time to waste.

CHAPTER 3

Principles

Now that you have read this far, you understand that complete family wealth goes far beyond money: it is the family's well-being, as encompassed by its qualitative capital—human, legacy, family relationship, structural, and social—and supported by its quantitative, financial capital. You know that flourishing families define themselves not by blood but by affinity and engage in a variety of practices to grow their qualitative and quantitative capital over time. You have seen that family enterprises recognize that management is just one circle of their concern, linked with responsible ownership and family connectedness over generations.

These ideas are the foundation for the rest of this book, in which we explore the who and the how of the journey of complete family wealth. At this point, as a tool to memory, here is a modified version of a table that Jay created over 20 years ago, one that many families have found useful to post in their boardrooms or at the head of their most important governance documents.

PRINCIPLES OF COMPLETE FAMILY WEALTH

I. Preservation of complete family wealth is a question of human behavior.

II. The most fundamental assets of a family are its individual members.

III. The complete wealth of a family includes the human, legacy, family relationship, structural, and social capital of its members. The family's financial capital is a tool to support the growth of its qualitative capital.

IV. To preserve its complete wealth successfully, a family must form a social compact among its members that reflects its shared values, and each generation must reaffirm and readopt that social compact.

V. To preserve its complete wealth successfully, a family must agree to create a system of representative governance through which it actively practices its values. Each generation must reaffirm its participation in that system of governance.

VI. The mission of family governance must be the enhancement of the pursuit of happiness of each individual family member. This pursuit will enhance the whole family and further the long-term preservation of the family's complete wealth: its qualitative as well as financial capital.

PART TWO

CHAPTER 4

The Rising Generation

Why Rising?

We begin this section on the *who* of family wealth with the rising generation. We do so purposefully. Most advisers and family members focus their attention on parents or grandparents. Explicitly or not they follow the supposed Golden Rule: whoever has the gold rules. That's usually the senior generation, the generation that has already risen to the height of family authority.

As an aside, if you are an adviser, ask yourself three questions: (1) Who is paying my fees? (2) Who do I consider my client? (3) Who is advocating for the growth and well-being of the rising generation? If the answers to those first two questions are, "the senior generation," and the third, "no one," then the family you are serving is heading for grief. If the answer to that third question is "someone other than me," then they likely won't be your clients for long.

If you are a member of the rising generation in a family, you know that you are the family's future. You hold the keys to the family's true wealth.

That's why we use the term *rising*. More often, people refer to the "next" generation in families with wealth or a family business. We recommend that you eliminate the term *next* from your vocabulary, at least as it refers to generations. "Next" puts the emphasis on what came first and, again, that's parents or the wealth creators; they are the important ones; everyone else is just next.

In contrast, we believe that each generation has its promise. Each generation has its ability to rise. This capacity is most evident when members of the rising generation are young adults or people in their 20s or 30s. But "rising" also does not need to be limited to age or demography (e.g., millennials or Gen Xers). Many times, especially within families with wealth, people in their 40s, 50s, or 60s who never had a chance to fully establish their own identities are taking hold of the opportunity to rise.

We are now going to focus on rising in early adulthood; we will return at the end of the chapter to rising in the middle passage of life.

The Effects of the Black Hole

Rising and growing are a part of human life, whether you live amid great financial capital or not. But, as we just mentioned, sometimes the presence of great financial capital can impede the natural tendency to rise.

We capture the source of this danger in an image we call the "Black Hole." If you come from a family of significant wealth, think for a moment about your history. Is there someone who looms large, as the creator of the family's good fortune? Do you as a family tell admiring stories about this person's trials and triumphs? Do his or her values and views dominate family decisions? Do his or her decisions about trusts or partnerships still shape family members' choices about how they live their lives?

If so, your family is not unusual. The larger-than-life founder is a fixture in most families with significant wealth. Such a founder and his or her dream can serve as a sun to the entire family, shining upon its members, making possible good things, and giving the family a sense of belonging and importance.

At the same time, it is precisely this amazing founder and his or her dream that we call the Black Hole. For next to this person's accomplishments and dreams, everyone else in the family, for generations, can seem to shrink to insignificance.

The fundamental question that faces any member of the rising generation, then, is, "How can I escape the gravity of the Black Hole and establish my own sense of identity and pursue my own dreams?"

To begin to think through that question, it is important to be clear about yourself and about the effects that the Black Hole may already have on you. Here are some characteristics that we often see crop up in families with significant wealth. As you read through them, do any of them describe you or members of your family?

- The Dutiful Steward: stewardship and tradition are good things. But sometimes they seem to take the place of everything else. If you are only a steward, what are you? Whose dream are you stewarding? What about your own dreams?
- The Meteor: How many times have we met members of the rising generation who tell us that they found out about the staggering size of their families' wealth when they mistakenly got financial statements in the mail! The effect of such disclosures can be like a meteor crashing into the recipient's atmosphere. The member of the rising generation can be knocked totally off course, wondering who he or she is and what path in life is worth pursuing. The effect of the meteor is even more powerful if the Black Hole has silenced all discussions of family wealth before then.
- Froggy: the proverbial frog placed in a pot of hot water jumps right out, while one in a slowly heated pot gets cooked. Are you being slowly cooked by the attractions—nice houses, great vacations, lots of toys—of the Black Hole? Do you want to jump but worry about how cold it might be outside?
- The Parallel Universe: We have known parents who, in a mistaken attempt perhaps to free themselves from the Black Hole's gravity, purposefully brought their children up shopping at Goodwill or Salvation Army, even though they had millions of dollars in financial assets. When, inevitably, those members of the rising generation found out, they felt betrayed, as though their childhood had been lived in a parallel universe. They were left wondering, perhaps permanently, "What's real?"
- The Anxious Heir: "Compared to the founder, how can I ever measure up?" That's a worry many members of the rising generation nurse in their hearts. It can lead to feeling always unsure about your own ability to make good decisions, trust others, and manage your own life.
- Mr. Reputable: A common variant of this anxiety takes the form of worrying about the family's reputation and severely limiting your own choices—of where to live, what to do, which friends to have—with a view toward "keeping up the good name."
- The Grand Giver: Some members of the rising generation seek to blast out of the orbit of the Black Hole by openly repudiating their family's wealth, perhaps by giving it all away philanthropically. Such giving may do some good in the world, but it can lead to deep regrets and broken family relationships.

The Challenge

The solution to the problem posed by the Black Hole is psychological, captured in the word "individuation." This means establishing your own sense of identity as an individual with skills, knowledge, character, and purpose. It means separating your identity from the identities of the founder, your parents, teachers, and other important influencers on your life.

Individuation takes place within the context of development. To provide an outline of human development, we have summarized the psychoanalyst Erik Erikson's account of its main stages. Each stage is characterized by a *dilemma* and activities appropriate to addressing that dilemma:

- Infant
    Trust vs. Mistrust
    Needs maximum comfort with minimal uncertainty to trust herself, others, and the environment.
- Toddler
    Autonomy vs. Shame and Doubt
    Works to master physical environment while maintaining self-esteem.
- Preschooler
    Initiative vs. Guilt
    Begins to initiate, not imitate, activities; develops conscience and sexual identity.
- School-Aged Child
    Industry vs. Inferiority
    Tries to develop a sense of self-worth by refining skills.
- Adolescent
    Identity vs. Role Confusion
    Tries integrating many roles (child, sibling, student, athlete, worker) into a self-image under role model and peer pressure.
- Young Adult
    Intimacy vs. Isolation
    Learns to make personal commitment to another as spouse or partner.
- Middle-Aged Adult
    Generativity vs. Stagnation
    Seeks satisfaction through productivity in career, family, and civic interests.

- Older Adult
  Integrity vs. Despair
  Reviews life accomplishments, deals with loss and preparation for death.

Before going on, ask yourself these questions:

- What stage of adult development are you in right now?
- What stage of development are your significant family members in?
- What special challenges are you experiencing in your present stage of development?
- What did you do that was most helpful in making life transitions in the past?
- You could better enjoy your present stage of life if you would continue . . . ?
- You could better enjoy your present stage of life if you would stop . . . ?
- You could better enjoy your present stage of life if you would start . . . ?

Individuation is an activity that transcends several of the stages of life, especially from childhood through middle age. Very importantly, individuation does not mean individualism—losing all connection to where you came from and other members of your family. It means maintaining a mature connection with others. It involves a balance of separateness and connectedness, or independence and interdependence. That's a balance that each one of us must find, with wealth or without wealth. It is a basic human challenge.

To that basic human challenge, add the special factor or special need of family wealth. Family financial capital has a way of emphasizing connectedness. If you have successful parents, it can be hard to get out from under their shadow. If your family is famous, it can be hard to establish your own name. If you grow up surrounded by trusts and businesses and the like, you may find it tough to make your own choices about important topics in your life.

In truth, at different points in your life, the founding dream may appropriately loom larger, at other points smaller. It is never possible—or even desirable—for either part, your dream or your family's connectedness, to vanish completely.

Many members of the rising generation tell us that their parents worry that they will become entitled. But the real cause of entitlement is the failure of the rising generation to individuate. The core of entitlement is failing to see yourself as a capable, independent person. The antidote to entitlement is individuation.

Meeting the Challenge

Rising is a life's work. Here are two suggestions on how to continue or begin the process:

1. Ask yourself, "In which situations have I felt truly in control, positively committed, gladly challenged, and in community with others?" These "Four Cs" indicate a place of self-centeredness and self-efficacy. Recognizing where you feel the Four Cs can help you seek out similar situations in the present and future (see Figure 4.1). (For more on the Four Cs, see the Conclusion.)
2. Next, think about what activities you are good at. What do you esteem about yourself? Where have you enjoyed the greatest success? You decide what success means. Once you've identified these activities, look behind them: what strengths have allowed you to enjoy this success?

These are questions aimed at self-knowledge. But self-knowledge does not come only, or for all people, from reflection. It can also come from action. It is important to test your self-understanding in practice.

The areas that we have found most important in that testing are *work*, *relationships*, and *communication* (especially with other family members, including parents). If there are any red flags that our experience has taught us to look out for in families with significant wealth, they are when children grow up without any true sense of work (done by themselves or their parents), without lasting and trusting relationships, and without open and honest communication in the family.

In the pages that follow you will find specific chapters devoted to the subjects of work, friendships, and communication. Here we will summarize a few points about each especially relevant to the rising generation.

FIGURE 4.1   The Four Cs.

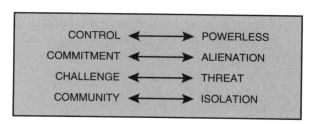

When it comes to work, look for activities that challenge you and test your abilities, that require your dedication, and that also meet the true needs of others. That work may be for pay; it may be voluntary. It may be part- or full-time. The key is that in having to dedicate ourselves at least in part to others' needs, we learn a great deal about our own strengths.

If you are growing up in the context of an operating business controlled by your family, there may be a strong incentive for you to work in that business. This can be a wonderful experience, but we recommend that you pursue it only after you have had significant experience, say, three to five years, testing yourself and growing through work someplace else. You will make contacts and learn skills and knowledge perhaps unavailable at home, making you even more valuable to the family enterprise. Further, you (and your family) will never feel bedeviled by the question of whether you could make it on your own outside the proverbial nest.

As for relationships, we recommend that members of the rising generation (or indeed any generation) cultivate relationships with people who:

- Affirm your strengths.
- Share your dreams.
- Are positive and forward-focused.
- Challenge you to be the best you can be.

Think about your own close friendships or other relationships. Can you see elements of these characteristics in your friends or partners? One of the main concerns voiced by members of the rising generation within families with wealth is that they fear that prospective friends or partners will see them only for their money. This is a valid concern. The response to this challenge is not to hide your money, much less to flaunt it, but to go beyond the money in evaluating your prospective friends. If they do the four things listed above, you will find ways together to deal with the money.

Finally, when it comes to communication within your family about wealth, here are a few points to consider:

- Accept that talking about family wealth is hard, but don't wait for your parents or grandparents to bring it up. They may not know how to.
- Think about what you would like to learn and why. Try to make your questions as specific as possible. For example, "What are your expectations for how I will use any financial inheritance I may receive?" "What are your hopes for me regarding work and income, saving and spending?" "Do you

expect me to join the family business or continue certain other traditions as part of my receiving this financial capital?"

- Think about who your parents or grandparents are, and how best to approach them. One-on-one? In the context of a family meeting? With a written note first to give them a chance to think?

Again, work, relationships, and communication are three areas in which we have seen members of the rising generation truly discover their strengths, weaknesses, and areas for growth. It is from such activities and self-reflection that something truly fundamental arises: clarity about your *dreams*. We have heard many parents tell us, "I don't know what my children's dreams are." We have heard many members of the rising generation say, "I haven't found my dreams!" Sometimes this emphasis on dreams can seem like a burden. One might feel like a failure if one's dreams aren't crystal clear. Our experience is that dreams become clear only with time, with effort, and as the result of a process of growth and exploration. They are almost never clear at the beginning of that process.

To offer you encouragement and inspiration in pursuing your dreams, here are lines from two poems, both of which speak to the journey of that great explorer Odysseus, himself a larger-than-life leader. The first comes from the Greek poet C.P. Cavafy's poem *Ithaca*:

> When you set off on the road to Ithaca
>> pray that the road be long,
>> full of adventures, full of knowledge.

Ithaca is the place we all want to get to, the object of our aspirations and hopes. Most people focus on the destination and want to get there already. But the rising is the journey.

The second comes from the Russian-born poet Joseph Brodsky's poem *Odysseus to Telemachus*, which imagines Odysseus speaking to his son, Telemachus, who himself faced the challenge of rising in the shadow of such a great father:

> Grow up, then, my Telemachus, grow strong . . .
>> Your dreams, my Telemachus, are blameless.

> Your dreams, too, are blameless.

Rising in the Middle Passage

As we mentioned when we defined the term "rising," it is not only young adults in their 20s and 30s who are rising. Every generation can rise. In the context of great financial wealth, we often see rising delayed until members are in the middle passage of life, in their 30s, 40s, or even 50s. Rising at this point includes everything we have discussed already, plus some special considerations.

One of those considerations, to return to Erikson's stages of development, is that the challenge involves not only individuation but also facing the dilemma of stagnation versus generativity. Life can become routine. It can feel as though the past and regrets outweigh the future and hope. The antidote to such stagnation is generativity: a sense of giving back, distilling what you have learned and experienced, and using it for the benefit of others (your children, nieces and nephews, or other members of your community). Generativity is often key to the rising of family members in the middle passage.

To do so, it can help to seek the support and insights of others in your shoes. These may be other family members, such as siblings or cousins. They may be members of other families with significant wealth, who you can meet through membership organizations, philanthropic boards, or the like. The middle passage can be isolating for anyone, especially if surrounded by large financial capital. Use your networks to break down that isolation and practice *active ownership* that we discussed in Chapter 2. Taking active ownership may involve making your voice heard in the management of your financial capital and directing it to investments that suit your values. It may also involve taking a more active hand in bringing your larger family together to communicate, learn, and make decisions. Active ownership of your life may entail even larger steps, such as leaving a career or a relationship that feels stifling. Whatever the case may be, the middle passage is a time when it is crucial to ask whether you are leading your life or a life that you think others want for you.

Setting Off

Before closing this chapter, let's return to the journey of rising generally.

With this journey in mind, here is a list of questions to reflect upon. If you have a coach or mentor, they are also great questions to get that individual's reflections on, based on that person's knowledge of you. If you are coaching a member of the rising generation, perhaps a child or niece or nephew, asking them to reflect on such questions can form the basis of meaningful conversations:

- Am I free or am I dependent?
- Have I found meaningful work?
- Am I a good friend?
- Can I feel compassion for myself?
- Can I express gratitude?
- Can I experience joy and humor?
- Have I taken part in larger civil society? In giving to others?
- In which areas do I want to grow further?

This list of questions can feel daunting. If it does, then take on a few at a time, perhaps covering the whole list over the course of six months or a year. The idea behind them is to be intentional about your rising.

CHAPTER 5

The Big Reveal

Confirmation

Most young adults in families with significant wealth go through something like what's called in the field "the talk" or even more dramatically "the Big Reveal."

In the stereotypical version, the 18- or 21-year-old is ushered into a lawyer's or wealth manager's office. The professional may begin with a few pleasantries and questions about school or work or travels. Then, after a pause and a bit of throat-clearing, the lawyer or financial adviser will say that the adult child's parents thought it important that he or she know certain things and from there launch into a speech about how the family has enjoyed great good fortune, and that with that good fortune comes responsibilities, such as management, oversight, philanthropy, etc.

Then, while the young adult continues to sit politely but mutely, the professional will flip through a variety of spreadsheets, flowcharts, and the like, moving along quickly but not too quickly. Yet everything the professional says is a blur after the recipient has seen the number at the bottom line. Once the charts are done, the lawyer or adviser might ask for questions, but what are you going to ask? The most relevant question—when and how can I get hold of some of this money?—seems terribly impolite. And a sharp-witted recipient can guess that any answer would likely be shrouded in mysterious complexity. So the meeting ends with a return to pleasantries, which a half hour before seemed matter-of-fact but now feel bizarre.

This is the stereotypical version, but like many stereotypes, it happens quite frequently. The details may differ. More communicative families may schedule the "Big Reveal" to take place alongside a family meeting, so that the young adult meets with the family's team of advisers. Other families dribble out the information, perhaps using visual charts—with no numbers attached—to illustrate the family's estate plans to teenagers, and fill in the numbers only when the recipients are in their early 20s. Each step is part of the "Big Reveal."

Parents and grandparents and their advisers worry a lot about the "Big Reveal." They may spend many hours or days planning it. But the truth is that, usually, the "Big Reveal" is not much of a reveal. Most children, even very young children, know if their families have money. Most children in families with money know that their parents are rich and that they enjoy various privileges as a result of this financial wealth. Thanks to the Internet, many of these children have very specific information about the financial value of their parents' homes, vehicles, businesses, etc.

The "Big Reveal," then, is more of a *confirmation*. All those stories that swirled around your childhood—those garbled half-speeches that your parents gave you about good fortune and opportunity and responsibility—the witty advice, "Don't put your trust in money, put your money in trust!"—the admiring or envious comments by friends and classmates or even teachers—suddenly, it all turns out to be true. You will be, or are, rich. The "reveal" makes it *real*. After it, you may go around in a daze for a while. You may look at everyday things and people in a new light. No matter how well-prepared you are by good character or financial literacy or work experiences—to use the image that flies through this book—the "Big Reveal" is a "meteor." Its true impact may become evident only years or decades later, when the actual "reveal" is at best a hazy memory, papered over by a multitude of meetings and documents, plans and projects.

So, as information, the reveal may not be anything new. But it can still be big. Not so much a "Big Reveal," but a Big Deal.

As advisers, we can't say how many times parents, grandparents, and their advisers have asked us when to hold the "Big Reveal." How old should the recipients be? 18? 21? 25? Later? Earlier? They also ask us what to say, and how to say it, and where. And they certainly ask us what to do or say or teach to prepare recipients for the "Big Reveal."

And yet, none of us recall anyone ever asking, "What do we do after the 'Big Reveal'?" That's what this chapter is about. Because what happens after the "Big Reveal" makes all the difference.

What's Next?

To begin to understand this point, step back for a moment from the event, the "Big Reveal," and think about its content. How can any of us imagine what it is to be given millions or tens of millions of dollars—or more? Far from imagining what it's like beforehand, it's hard to understand it when it's happening. As mentioned, the effects may become clear only years after the meteor has hit.

Likewise, how can anyone imagine what it is to *give* such huge sums? If you made your fortune, you probably know lots about giving people opportunities, giving them your trust, giving them your time, and insights, and attention or praise. But just giving money away, not paying? If you've had to make it for yourself, you'll likely have less experience in that.

Conversely, if you grew up amid wealth and were given it by your parents or grandparents, you may have lots of experience in receiving. But not so much in giving.

Still, it is generally harder for a recipient to receive than a giver to give. Why is that? It seems counterintuitive. Most people enjoy receiving; some grumble about giving, especially large gifts. Little children don't need to be taught how to eat their cake; they need to be taught to share it. Nonetheless, the task of giving well is easier than that of receiving well. If the giver made his or her money, then he or she probably loves it—wealth or a business is like a child—but he or she also feels in control of it. He or she is free to give. It's *his* or *hers*, so he or she can make it *yours*, as he or she sees fit. And if the giver finds himself or herself wanting more, he or she can make more. The giver who received wealth may have a harder time giving it away than the one who made it, since, as one heir we knew put it, "It's all I'll ever have." Still, if this inheritor has a great deal, more than enough, then he or she can give some of the surplus away, and leave the rest upon death. To someone who is used to receiving, money doesn't mean that much. It has always been there.

So, despite the universal lack of preparation, these givers have an easier row to hoe than the recipient of significant sums. Their challenge is to perform a certain action well, to *give* well. The recipient's challenge goes beyond receiving: the recipient's challenge is to *live* well. Most givers have already established their ways of life. What is the recipient's to be? That is the question. And it's a big one.

Is the recipient to pursue making money, like his or her father or mother or whoever it was who is revered as the "founder of the family"? But why, if he or she has already been given a fortune? But he or she may still persist because he or she loves some lucrative field or other, but still the question will nag—the question of "Why?"—and it may weaken him or her in comparison to competitors. Or maybe the recipient wants to pursue some other life, in art or study or politics or adventure. But will that be so? All worthy lives require *dedication*, hard work. Great money beckons to its possessors to take it easy and enjoy life. It loosens ambition. It softens the desires and the spirit—at least in most cases. It poses great challenges to the recipient, for he or she has not just a good gift to make: he or she has a good life to make.

The Pause

So what is the recipient to do? Our answer is: take a pause. With regard to the *money*. But not with regard to *life*. The words we would hope the recipient learns, with regard to family financial capital, are "Not Yet."

As in the stereotypical scene with which we began this chapter, most recipients are in their early 20s when they get the "Big Reveal." Yes, let it happen then. But then let the recipient have nothing to do with the money. Let him or her respond, "Not yet," to invitations to get more engaged. No monthly statements. No meetings with trustees. No joining this or that family committee or Family Council or a Junior Board or the like. Tell the recipient that he or she can say "Not yet," and not have anything to do with the money for as long as he or she likes—10 years even. If the recipient wants a distribution for some reason or other that is really important and can't get the funds elsewhere, you or the trustees will consider it—but with no promises. He or she should live life as if the money doesn't exist.

But of course it does. And the recipient knows that it does. And so, during this time, this pause toward money but not toward life, the recipient will face his or her true dragons. What will he or she do? That is the question.

Some recipients **fight** the dragons; they may want to give away the money, or devote it to causes that alleviate inequality, to express their disapproval of having more. Others **flee** it, pretend it isn't there. Many simply **freeze**: they don't ignore it but they don't take action, either. Fight, flight, or freeze are perfectly natural reactions to such a meteor.

In the midst of this trial, many others will come forward with a variety of "shoulds": you should do this, you should do that. "Should" is a wonderful word; it implies a command, a morality, a belief about what's right, without ever having to explain the grounds of that command.

To help the recipient most, the giver and others must sit back and watch. This is the recipient's life, not theirs. He or she must create it. No one can predict what someone will make before they make it. It is his or her continent to explore or landscape to paint. Before he or she embarks on this endeavor, nobody can be sure how it will turn out. The recipient faces freedom—which can be exhilarating and frightening. It is easy to retreat, to withdraw, into waiting or becoming a permanent student or signing up to be a "steward." For it can be hard to figure this out: what to *dedicate* yourself to when you know that you have the economic freedom to dedicate yourself to *nothing*.

Yes, it is hard—but we have seen it done. We knew a farmer who, though an odd coincidence of deaths in the family, in his late 20s inherited hundreds of millions of dollars from a distant relative. But he remained a farmer. He loved his life. He didn't have quite the same worries as his neighbors about the weather or the price of tractor parts. But he didn't need or want frills. He lived well below his means, but not by rejecting the money or by hiding from it. Rather, that's what his chosen life required. We knew another heir who was a successful sculptor. He led a comfortable life, due to his inherited wealth, but he did not let that comfort take him away from his studio. We've known many academicians who inherited significant wealth. They enjoy more luxurious vacations than their colleagues and are able to buy homes with ease. But otherwise the money doesn't matter that much to them. They live their lives as well as they can.

It's not uncommon for recipients to feel confusion and distress in their very bones—it is a somatic experience, not just an intellectual one. The meteor can be seen as a sort of trauma, which comes with its own post-traumatic stress. But this is an occasion for ready recipients to seek post-traumatic growth: to move beyond the reaction of fight, flight, or freeze, and to use this experience to learn more about themselves, their true wishes and desires, their limitations and their aspirations—to move toward **flourishing**.

That is the key—that is what ideally happens during this pause: the recipient learns to live *his* or *her* life, the life that is good for him or her. The recipient does so not in *ignorance* of the money, nor by pretending that it's not there. Neither does he or she *pursue* money if he or she doesn't want to—as if receiving money *requires* that you prove your merit by making more money. No, the recipient leads his or her life by whatever demanding standards of excellence it entails. Even if the task is to tend his or her own garden at home, the recipient will seek to do that well, for it is *his* or *her* life. That is what matters. The life, not the money.

That's the lesson that a recipient must learn during the pause. That is the point of the pause. In this respect, families today can use longevity to their advantage. In the past, a young heir or heiress might need to take responsibility for the family's affairs at any moment. Family histories abound with stories of 20-somethings who had to take the reins of a family business because of war or sudden illness and death. Today, heirs or heiresses might come into their complete property only in their 60s or even 70s. Thanks to the professionalization of the financial industry and good legal plans, they may face little need to manage the wealth. Use those formative years well—the 20s, even 30s or 40s. If you are a recipient, live *your* life. Know that the money is there, in the background. But this is how you "integrate" it, into *your* life.

This "integration" is the point of a story that St. Ignatius tells in his *Spiritual Exercises*, a story of three people, each of whom received a large sum of money. (Ignatius himself grew up in a wealthy family, so he knew whereof he spoke.) The first person, Ignatius says, eagerly spent the money on things he wanted and then lamented the loss of the money. The second person, in contrast, pushed the money as far away from himself as possible, hiding it or even giving it away. The third person chose a different path. He neither spent the money nor gave it away. Instead, he did what he did with the money based on what his own life's purpose was. He determined the money's use; it did not determine him.

To do this, to take this third path, requires *resolve*. It takes resolve against the pleasures and luxuries that money can buy. It takes resolve in the face of fear of the money, of screwing it up or letting it "change" you and so twisting yourself in knots by trying to run away from it. It takes resolve not to make your life about the money—as a would-be money-maker, or as a dutiful steward, or as a showy spender. Most importantly, it takes the resolve to seek out and to choose and to stick to what you see as the best life available to you.

People show this kind of resolve when they are buying a car or a house. Why then should it be so hard when it comes to choosing a life? Why do we need encouragement—literally, to have courage put in us—when it comes to seeking and leading a good life, a life that is good for us? Part of the reason is that the bribes that money offers are large. There is the bribe to give into softness. There is the bribe to yoke yourself to a sense of "responsibility" through "stewardship." But another reason is that a truly excellent life—whether as a farmer or artist or teacher or the like—is not just hard but *risky*: you stake your all on this throw. However, the fact remains that we toss the dice one way or another. Each of must choose how to live. Even if you don't have to take on paid work, because you do not face economic necessity, you cannot evade this choice, the choice of how to live.

Pursuing this search with resolve is all the harder for those who have grown up amid luxuries and perhaps also in the shadow of famous, highly successful parents or grandparents. Such recipients have probably heard many times that "To whom much is given, much will be required." They feel that expectation both because of who they are descended from and because of what they can expect to receive. Many such recipients feel that they should live up to these expectations, that they should prove that they deserve to be given so much. The money looms large. Should they try to prove themselves by seeking more? Or turn their hand to managing and stewarding what they've been given? Either path can be a wonderful journey for someone for whom that's the right way. Either path can be a trap for someone who was meant to lead a very different life.

Courage

So, extend that pause, continue to say, "Not yet," as long as possible. If you are a parent, let your recipients be in their 40s if possible before they start coming to board meetings or talking with trustees or asking for trust distributions. Let them have well-established lives. Not because you did not tell them the truth. But *despite* that tempting truth.

Anyone of us can choose to pursue flourishing, regardless of money. A recipient of significant wealth has a harder time to seek and pursue a life that is not all about money. That said, the recipient also has the opportunity to lead the sort of good life that *requires* money: that does good things that cannot be done *without money*. Still, the question is not whether the recipient *can* do such things—of course, he or she has the resources—but rather *are these activities his or her destined path*? Don't be a philanthropist merely because you have money. Be a farmer or an artist or a teacher if that's what you were meant to be.

The value of the pause is that the recipient learns about himself or herself, and learns to continue that process of learning. Experience teaches the recipient a learning mindset, which will prove invaluable in all stages and activities of life.

Of course, if you want to pursue the activities that can be done well *only* with money, there are teachers who can teach you how to do these better rather than worse. But who will help you lead *your* life, *without regard to the money*? Or, as Ignatius puts it, with "proper indifference" to the money?

This helper we imagine as an old man sitting beneath a tree, as the recipient stands nearby, gazing out over the continent that is or will be his or her life. The old adviser isn't there to teach the recipient about that continent. How could he? The old man doesn't know what that life will look like. Not even the recipient knows what that life will look like. Nor is the old man there to teach the recipient certain skills or give him or her specific tools. Again, how would the old man know what tools or skills the recipient will need? And even if he did know, the old man might not possess those skills or tools himself.

The old man is there, as we put it before, to encourage the recipient. To give him or her courage. To pursue this unknown, unknowable, exciting but frightening attempt. To give color to this work, we like to return to that image of froggy, the frog in the cooking-pot. We all know that wealth can cook a young heir or heiress, by slowing offering its bribes and sapping the recipient's spirit. But most of us don't think about the risks inherent in the jump from the pot. That frog might think, "What if I land in the fire?" Or, "This pot is pretty nice—what if the world out there isn't so nice?" The frog cannot know the world outside the pot until and after he jumps and his choice is made. The old man sitting by the tree gives the recipient the courage to take that leap. The old man does so by sitting by the recipient's side in profound compassion, being with the recipient, and acknowledging the challenging, risky, and rewarding future that lies before him or her.

As such, this old man—and he doesn't have to be literally an old man; he could be a she, or even a youngish man or woman—straddles the life that the recipient knew before he or she jumped and the life after. The old man by the tree also may be one of the few people in the recipient's life who knows the truth about the money. The old man by the tree is the preserver, the defender, of the pause—the pause with regard to the money, which gives room for life. As such, the old man by the tree is your reminder of the money. But he is a safe reminder: neither alluring nor frightening. Most of all, he reminds you to look to *you*. Because he knows about the money, and what it could mean, he can keep reminding you *not* to focus on it, to focus on *yourself*.

CHAPTER 6

Parents

Giving

In this chapter, we consider the role of being a parent within a family with significant wealth. We consider that role from the standpoint of a fundamental activity: giving.

Gifts are the lifeblood of family. Parents give their children care, education, a place to live, clothes to wear, and so much more. In families with significant wealth, gifts play a large but often undiscussed role. They may take the forms of annual exclusion gifts, gifts of tuition, trust interests, shares in a business, and bequests. How these gifts are given may determine whether children go on to live happy, fulfilled lives or whether they lead lives of subsidy, dependency, and entitlement.

The key to giving wisely is to recognize that every true gift carries something more than money or property. It carries *spirit*. Though intangible, the spirit of the gift makes all the difference. As the Roman philosopher Seneca wrote 2,000 years ago, "As a gift is given, so shall it be received." Is it any surprise that gifts that are made grudgingly are not received gratefully? Or gifts that are truly tax-minimization strategies are not treated as instances of generosity?

Often the spirit expresses the giver's intention: for example, to further the recipient's education, to provide a beautiful place to live and raise a family, or to remind the recipient of the love of a living or deceased relative. True gifts promote the growth and freedom of both giver and recipient.

But most of our supposed gifts are not true gifts. They are *transfers*. Transfers lack spirit. They move assets from one balance sheet to another. They often leave both giver and recipient feeling that there are strings attached. Repeated over time, transfers weaken recipients' identity, undermine their independence, and lead to subsidy or entitlement.

Even though most gifts start out as transfers, they don't need to end up that way. Transfers can be transformed into gifts. The rest of this chapter summarizes some lessons that can help you make that transformation—or to make true gifts right from the start.

Know Thyself

Making gifts with spirit starts with asking the right questions. When most people think about giving, they start with *what* they want to give (cash, stocks, bonds, a car, the vacation house, etc.). Or they move quickly to asking *how* they should give (outright, in trust, through loans, etc.). These are the sorts of questions that occupy much of estate planning.

The reason is that many of these planning conversations focus on reducing taxes. This is a fine goal, as far as it goes. But it does not touch upon the ultimate purposes and the consequences of the gift. Focusing just on saving taxes can result in what looks momentarily like a win feeling like a long-term loss.

The most important question to begin with is not what or how but *who*. Start with the people rather than the property or the process. Begin with yourself, the giver: who are you?

"Know thyself" is the maxim to adopt. Some questions that help toward that goal include:

- What do you want to achieve with this gift?
- Does it reflect your values?
- Does it bring you joy?

It is simple to pose these questions but often challenging to think them through. Give yourself the time and space to express, reflect on, and understand your motivations for giving.

Sometimes we feel remorse after making gifts. "What have I done?" is an exclamation we have heard from many family members, sometimes moments after signing planning documents, sometimes months or even years down the road. This "grantor's remorse" is painful, but we can also learn from it. It often points to the need to begin educating recipients about the transfers that are coming their way.

Another feeling givers need to attend to is guilt. Some gifts come from love. Others proceed from guilt. Perhaps the givers feel they didn't give recipients enough time or affection. Perhaps they want to make up for past hurts. You don't need to judge these feelings, but it is crucial to surface and address them. Gifts made from guilt leave neither the giver nor the recipient feeling good.

Nothing Too Much

The next "who" to consider in the cycle of the gift is the recipient. Many financial transfers treat the recipients as afterthoughts. Recipients are considered passive. They may be young and still unformed. They may not even be born. But to give wisely, you need to attend to the recipients. Giving is like a game of catch: How can you know whether to throw hard or soft, long or short, if you have no idea who you're throwing to?

To use an image from Chapter 4, every gift is like a meteor flying from the giver to the recipients. These meteors enter recipients' atmospheres and have an impact. The question is what your meteor contains. Is it love? Is it guilt? Is it freedom or control? The answer to those questions will make a huge difference as to whether your recipients can integrate the meteor into their lives.

Just as you should reflect on yourself as a giver, so, too, reflect on your recipients, with such questions as the following:

• What is the recipient's age and stage of development?
• What is the recipient's temperament?
• What about character—is the recipient's character formed or still developing?
• Do you trust the recipient?

The answers to these questions will allow you to start thinking through the secondary questions of what, when, and how to give. For example, if your recipients are very young or don't even exist yet, your next question may be who can serve as a trustee to carry on the spirit of your gift with these recipients someday?

How Much Is Enough? Fair versus Equal?

Thinking about who each recipient is leads naturally to two other very common questions: How much is enough for my children? And should I give an equal amount to each of them?

How much is a question whose answer depends on both the giver and the recipient. First, how much is enough for you? How much do you need to live? How much do you want to give to others (including charities) during your life? How much do you want to leave for your heirs? What kind of standard of living do you want to set? Unless you tell your children to expect differently, your choices—the cars you drive, the homes you live in, the places that you vacation—will shape their expectations. Once you have figured out how much is enough for you, then turn to asking, "How much?" for children or grandchildren, using the questions about recipients that we shared earlier.

Equality is another major consideration for families. Children have different abilities, aspirations, and needs. As a result, parents often give their children different levels of attention, care, and advice at different points in their lives. But when it comes to money or property, unequal giving easily leads to hurt feelings, resentment, and even conflict. That is why, unless special circumstances demand otherwise, we generally recommend that parents follow the path of equality in their financial gifts. In special cases, such as those involving a child's disability or dependency, there may be good reason for deviating from equality. In such cases, it is even more important to communicate your reasons early and clearly, so that there are no surprises down the road.

Communication and Control

Once you have gained some clarity about yourself and your recipients, perhaps the most important factor in giving wisely is communication. Gifts can't speak for themselves. That spirit of the gift requires communication to give it voice.

As George Bernard Shaw is supposed to have said, "The greatest enemy to communication is the illusion that it has taken place." True communication requires courage and intentionality.

Many parents ask, "When should I start telling my children about our wealth?" There is no one time nor is there just one message. In general, people wait too long and share too little, out of the fear of doing harm. Waiting is only natural, as we all want to do the best for our children and not make mistakes. (We share more specifics on communicating about wealth with younger children in Chapter 14.)

Despite these concerns, when it comes to young adult or adult children, we recommend that parents communicate more rather than less, sooner rather than later. The fact is, thanks to the internet, conversations with friends, and their own observations, most adolescents or young adults know more than their parents would like to admit. Waiting and keeping secrets carry a hefty opportunity cost. Sharing some information can be a chance to listen and to learn from your children's responses.

Of course, communicating well depends on preparation. Too often estate planning or giving turns into a series of down-to-the-wire emails and phone calls between family members and their advisers. It is hard to remember, much less communicate to others, matters that have happened in a flurry. If that has been your experience, then ask your advisers for a one-page summary of any new trust or plan or gift, with the key terms highlighted. Use that summary as the starting point for thinking through your communication.

Another step you can take with your advisers is to create an actual communication plan. Giving well is hard. Talking about your gifts with your children or grandchildren may be even harder. One way to reduce the difficulty is to craft a communication plan to share the news about the gift at the right time, in the right way, with the proper recipients. A good plan covers the content, the tone, and the process of communication. The communication plan doesn't need to be in place before the gift is finalized. But knowing that you have a resource to help you create that plan may help defuse any misgivings you have even before they arise.

Communication is one of the areas of giving that bring us face-to-face with the issue of control. Control is a huge issue for most givers. As one patriarch told us, "My children tell me that I am trying to control them from the grave. I tell them they're right!" Many givers believe that communication means ceding control.

This doesn't have to be the case. The key is to plan your communication so that you manage your disclosures and you learn from the process. For example, we often recommend that families start with sharing the existence of certain trusts and the information about how the trusts will work but hold off on sharing the numbers. The questions that your recipients ask or their reactions to what you share can then help you decide how much more to share and when.

Also, always remember that to discuss a matter is not the same as deciding it or delegating that decision to the recipients. When sharing your thinking about prospective gifts with your adult children, consider adding very clearly the caveat that you have not made any decisions and retain the prerogative to change your mind. Sharing your thinking before a gift is made can be a great way to judge whether the time, amount, and vehicles are all right for the recipients.

The same goes for making actual gifts. Start small. Learn from the recipient's actions to see whether he or she is ready for larger gifts. For example, one parent we know gave her daughter a gift of $10,000 when she began freshman year of college. This amount was meant to cover the young woman's expenses for the next four years. It lasted about four months. But rather than take her daughter to task, this mother reflected how unprepared she would have been if she had received such a sum at age 18. Together, they worked out a budget, a sense of reasonable expenses, and a plan for the daughter to get a job to cover these expenses.

This example points to a larger lesson for parents of children who are in the phase of life known as "emergent adulthood," roughly from 18 to their mid-20s. This is a time when children are exploring their independence while also relying somewhat on the security of school and the parental home. It is a difficult time to navigate, for all parents and children. Great financial wealth can make it even more trying. It is a time when many children are required by law to be notified of their trusts. It is also a time when many children receive and perhaps misspend significant gifts. If parents criticize emergent adults for these mistakes, the stigma can last a lifetime, impeding that young adult's ability to learn healthy ways of managing money. Instead, see this period as one of experimentation. Some experiments work. Others don't. We can learn from all of them.

Giving as Grandparents

Giving well as a grandparent involves complexities all its own.

For example, we once worked with a grandfather (whom we'll call Frank) who had three adult children and almost a dozen grandchildren. Frank had inherited significant wealth from his parents, who had founded a major business, in the form of several family trusts. He was considering how to restructure those trusts as part of his estate planning. He had come up with a plan to skip his children's generation and leave a significant amount of money to his grandchildren. By doing so, he would save a lot in taxes.

The technical aspects of his plan were sound. So we asked how Frank's plans fit with his values. He was a very independent man. Above all, he valued autonomy. "How," we asked, "does this plan fit with autonomy?" He thought for a moment and then realized that he was making a transfer that would make a huge impact on his grandchildren's lives, without even once discussing it with his children, his grandchildren's parents.

Frank's example highlights some important lessons for grandparents who want to give wisely:

1. As in the case of any gift, be clear about your own values. Then ask whether your actions are consistent with your values.
2. Communication with your children is crucial. How would you feel if not only the money but also the chance to determine its best use skipped you? Your children and their spouses will likely have more of an impact on your grandchildren's use of that money—for good or for ill—than you will. As much as you can, make them your partners in helping to increase the chances that it has a positive impact.
3. Learn from your children and their spouses. They probably know your grandchildren best. Engage them in a conversation about what would truly benefit each grandchild. In Frank's case, these conversations led him to make some of his gifts outright and others in trust. Because he engaged his children and their spouses in these discussions, everyone was clear about why he made his different choices.

Remember that engaging adult children in conversations about their children's best interests does not mean you cede to them the right to make your decisions for you.

One more practical point, which we will have more to say about in Chapter 18: tell stories. Grandparents are natural storytellers. Those stories forge bonds among generations and make the family's values concrete. They are even more important if they give descendants a sense of the hard work that created the family's wealth. Long before grandchildren learn the dollar value of their trusts, they can benefit from hearing stories about the work and care—the failures as well as triumphs—that have made their family what it is.

Letting Go

Even if you take all these steps, it's natural to worry about making a significant gift. Gifts are powerful. You cannot know what all the consequences will be. Part of giving wisely, then—like parenting generally—is to acknowledge the reality that we cannot control everything we would like to. We can only control what we say, what we do, and how we respond to events. The greatest control comes from having the confidence that, come what may, you can handle it.[1]

---

[1] For more on parenting amid wealth, consider *A Wealth of Possibilities* by Ellen Miley Perry (Washington, DC: Egremont Press, 2012), Chapter 2, "Be a Great Parent."

CHAPTER 7

Spouses

Tough Questions

It is hard enough to talk about money. Talking about love and money raises the difficulty exponentially. This is the challenge faced by spouses within the context of significant wealth.

In this chapter, we will address this challenge with respect to several particularly difficult situations: dealing with fiscal inequality, clarifying wishes in estate planning or giving, and making choices in the context of a blended family. Later, in Chapter 15, we will address the use of prenuptial agreements.

Fiscal Difference

In many marriages in the context of significant wealth, one partner comes to the marriage with—or creates during the marriage—much more financial capital than the other. Traditionally, this partner was usually the man. Thanks to demographic and social changes, that partner is now often the woman. In either case, the couple must manage the stresses caused by fiscal difference.

Usually, they must do so without much in the way of support. While there are many marriage counselors, few feel equipped to help couples deal with fiscal difference. And it is a topic that is deeply difficult to address head on. That is because the person who has more financial capital often approaches the topic with a mixture of guilt and fear: guilt at having more, and fear of being taken advantage of.

What then can the couple do? There are two main keys to meet this challenge:

1. The presence of positive regard and empathy for each other.
2. Each party feels self-sufficient and competent.

Positive Regard and Empathy for Each Other

This is, of course, the basis for any relationship. To this end, sometimes respecting the taboo against talking about money early in relationships is a good thing. Not discussing money with prospective partners can allow relationships to grow and strengthen based on who you are rather than what you have or might have.

Along these same lines, it is also a good thing to start out life living on what you earn. This is a positive experience for individuals, to know that you can support yourself. It is also good for couples, as you learn to navigate choices about how you spend your time and navigate money choices together.

Most importantly, make sure to value all the contributions of both partners. The most important contributions are often not financial. In any situation of fiscal difference, empathy is a key part of the response.

Each Party Feels Self-Sufficient and Competent

On this point, again, each member of the couple should go through the process we described in Chapter 4. The true basis for self-sufficiency is self-understanding and identification of your strengths through work, quality relationships, and communication. If you're going to navigate relationships of fiscal inequality with others, the first thing is to clarify your own reality: not only what you have but who you are.

Each spouse should also feel reasonably knowledgeable about the family's finances. This may mean doing some independent learning about investing, going to seminars, or joining the larger family's business meetings. Both spouses should also feel that they can speak directly with the couple's financial advisers. Having that relationship is important not only for each spouse's sense of competence but also in case something should happen to one member of the couple, so that the other does not feel left in the dark.

Beyond these two keys, some of the other practices that we have seen help couples deal with the challenge of fiscal inequality include:

1. Honoring both families of origin around holidays, not just the side with financial capital.
2. Being proactive in addressing fiscal inequality when it arises, rather than letting it go underground.
3. Talking with other members of your families, such as in the context of a family meeting; they likely have important insights to share on this topic, which may have been shrouded in silence.

One of the common consequences of fiscal difference is that the partner with more financial capital may be asked by other family members with less to offer them loans or gifts or other forms of financial support. This can be deeply uncomfortable.

The first step in addressing the issue of offering financial support to family members with less is to talk together as a couple, to make sure that whatever you decide, you are united in your decision. Next, if you are going to act financially, be clear about your motivations. Is it your own need—to be liked or to get along or to not make waves—rather than the other's true need that is motivating you? Finally, be clear about the manner of your action and your goals. For example, are you making a gift or a loan? If it truly is a loan, make sure that the terms—how long it will take to be repaid, the interest charged if any—are set down in writing and both parties have a copy. Very often, however, family members will couch a gift as a loan to save face, since everyone knows that the so-called loan will never be repaid. That can be okay—as long as you do not later decide to renegotiate the unspoken terms and demand payment on this loan. Again, clarity before a commitment is made will save much grief down the road.

The Three-Step Process

With this empathic stance, a couple can begin to formulate a shared vision regarding wealth in their family and the choices it brings. Often the choices couples face center around estate planning and giving. Based on his work with dozens of families, our colleague Charles Collier, former senior philanthropic adviser at Harvard University, recommends a three-step approach to these very important conversations:[1]

1. Clarify your individual views.
2. Share your clarity with each other.
3. Then decide what else to do as a couple.

The first step is to clarify your individual values and dreams and the options that you see before you. Take this step individually. Spend some time with your laptop or paper and pencil and write down what you think is important. Don't self-edit based on what your partner may think. Too often communication breaks down or never gets started because we are trying to respond to someone else's views (or what we think are someone else's views) rather than getting clear about our own beliefs. Managing wealth as a couple requires that each member of the team have that clarity.

Once you have done that individual work, turn to step two. The goal here is to share your clarity with each other. You may not agree on all points. The key is to identify your differences, discuss them, and respect them. You may find that there are differences where you thought there were none and points of agreement that you did not expect to find.

The key to this step, of course, is *listening*. It is a hard skill to learn. We encourage each member of the couple to speak, without interruption, while the other listens. Then the one listening can ask clarifying questions—but not object or make points of his or her own. Only when one member has finished should the other take his or her turn to speak.

Many times, couples find that step two leads back to step one. Talking about putting money in trust for children, for example, reinvesting funds in the business, or buying a new home becomes an iterative process of thinking, sharing, and thinking some more.

The third step is forward-focused. Once you have identified what you each believe, a path forward will likely start to emerge. That path may not have been what either one of you would have predicted. It may mean delaying a choice or moving ahead more quickly than anticipated. It may

[1] Charles Collier, "Financial Inheritance as a Family Conversation," July 2011. Copies are available from Harvard University, Office of Development.

mean sharing information with your children or other family members or deciding to stay quiet and revisiting the topic at a future date. Whatever the choice of action or communication is, you will have come to it in a truly shared way.

Collier's three-step process is a powerful tool. It is not an easy one to use. It takes time and patience. But if you stick with it, it can greatly strengthen your relationship as a couple and your relationships with other family members, too.

To again recall George Bernard Shaw's supposed quip, "The greatest enemy to communication is the illusion that it has taken place." The three-step process provides a way to overcome that obstacle.

Spouses and Family Meetings

Earlier in this chapter we mentioned that it can be helpful to invite spouses to family meetings, so that both spouses feel reasonably informed about the larger family enterprise. This is particularly important if you have children, as choices made by their grandparents or extended family may impact them. Also, it is very hard for a spouse to be an effective partner in raising a child amid wealth if he or she has been excluded from learning about the family enterprise. You can't teach what you don't know.

For all these reasons, when families ask us, "Should we invite spouses to our family meetings?" we generally respond, "Of course." That response comes with some caveats. First, if you are the mother or father who is organizing the family meeting, it is a good idea to ask your adult children if they would like their spouses to be present. This request shows them respect vis-à-vis their marriages, and it gives them and their spouses time to think and talk about the pros and cons of the spouses joining the meeting.

If the answer is, "Yes," you don't need to start by having spouses join the entire meeting right away. Perhaps there are sections that are more general or educational as distinct from board meetings or executive sessions where more sensitive issues are discussed. As is the case for any family member, spouses should demonstrate their seriousness about the meetings by doing required prep work, showing up on time, being present, and joining in the discussion.

If families take these steps, the inclusion of spouses can be an enormously powerful force. As we said in Chapter 2, families that succeed long-term look at themselves as connected not by blood but by affinity. Doing so allows them to integrate the learning, drive, empathy, and other strengths of their in-laws.

Blended Families

Nothing is easy about blending families after divorce or the death of a parent, and dealing with stepchildren and money is hard. To have effective conversations about family wealth within this context, we recommend tailoring the three-step process to the contours of a blended family. Using this process helps spouses tackle the core issues while also managing their emotions.

Again, start with yourselves as a couple and your principles. In this case, your conversation can focus on such matters as how you feel about sharing some of your wealth with your second spouse and his or her children, what you think such an inheritance is meant to accomplish, and what concerns you have if your children must wait for an inheritance because of your second marriage. These questions can be very challenging to answer, so try to be patient with yourself and your partner in these conversations.

Then, in the second step, solicit the input of your children and stepchildren. How you do so will depend on your family's dynamics. Some parents invite all the children together in one conversation. Others proceed one child at a time. Still others invite each child to speak with his or her biological parent first and then with the couple together. Whichever way you proceed, the goal remains to listen to what the children want to say. Questions that Charles Collier recommended using to elicit their thoughts are: "What are your expectations for an inheritance? And, how do you view the purpose of an inheritance from your stepmom or stepdad?"

After becoming clear about your principles and plans as a couple, with input from your children, the goal of the third step is to communicate your plans. Again, how you do so—child by child or as a group—will depend on your family. The key is to make the process affirm them as respected members of the family and you as a loving couple.

We can't stress enough the importance of empathy when dealing with a blended family, empathy for each other as spouses and empathy for your children from prior marriages.

We also recommend following the basic rule, if possible, of addressing questions about your plans and purposes while all parties are still alive. Use your documents and occasions when you are together as a family to make your wishes clear.

CHAPTER 8

Elders

"Old Age Hath Yet Its Honor and Its Toil"

As people are living longer and healthier lives, family enterprises are more and more often multigenerational affairs. At the same time, many of our societies glorify youth, not age. This condition raises two questions:

1. What is the appropriate role for the family to give the senior generation?
2. How can the senior generation remain active in the family's affairs in ways that are appropriate to their seniority but allow their children a chance to grow and lead?

If you are an elder, what are the gifts you bring to your family enterprise? Each family will come up with its own answer to this question. However, we've seen some patterns, both in history and in practice, that indicate several possible roles for successful elders:

- To tell the family's stories.
- To remind family leaders to follow the family's agreed-upon rules and to reflect the family's values and goals in the process of governance.
- To effectively mediate internal family disputes.
- To conduct the family's rituals.

As an elder, your stories give the family a crucial gift: a sense of being distinct from any other family. If your family has a clear idea of its lineage, it will engage naturally in seven-generation thinking.

Elders also remind family leaders of the family's agreed-upon rules, values, and goals. Families often fall into habitual patterns and let important insights or practices languish. Elders, with their experience, serve as the family's memory, keeping past agreements and decisions alive.

The third gift that elders offer to families is to mediate family disputes. Whether in ancient tribes or in modern industrialized societies, human beings look to their elder statesmen to mediate conflict. Usually these elders help the parties take the dispute out of the frame of established alliances or legalistic processes so that matters can be tackled more informally and directly.

The fourth gift that elders bring is to conduct the family's rituals. Rituals combine play and seriousness, freedom and control. As such, rituals require not just administration but also ordination. They require someone who engenders respect—the authority that goes beyond a vote or a title—to conduct them.

A family may not yet have elders suited to these four tasks. As a result, we've often seen people from outside the family step in. These outsiders may be long-time family friends. Very often they're trusted advisers from legal, financial, or human services professions who know the family members well. Again, the most successful families are based on affinity, not blood. If your family has not yet grown its own elders, you may very well have these external elders working with you until a true elder emerges from your family members.

Like Ulysses in the Tennyson poem bearing his name, a line from which heads this chapter, too often elders feel superfluous. These four activities harness their considerable gifts for the good of families and themselves.

Characteristics

An elder is not simply an older person, although many elders are of advanced age. What truly makes an elder is the development of certain qualities. We summarize these qualities using these four D words: discernment, discretion, discipline, and discovery.

Discernment

Elders have the capacity to sift through complicated matters. This discernment involves suspending the inclination to jump to a conclusion or action. It involves seeing the similarities and differences between this situation and others. Discernment sets a model of careful thinking for the rest of the family.

Discretion

Elders see and hear much and say little. They listen. They know when to let the family system work out its issues on its own, without direction or force. They are patient. They also know when to intervene for the sake of the common good. While drawing on the wisdom of their own elders, elders weigh their words and actions with a view not just to today or this year but to the distant future.

Discipline

Elders have an internal sense of control. This internal control gives them a deep sense of freedom. It also allows them to stand up for the family's shared norms and rules. By disciplining themselves, they provide a model to others.

Discovery

Often through hard-won experience, elders know the central priority of assessment over action. They learn from each member of the family. They look for the differences among the members, the branches, and the larger family. They also look outside the family for sources of wisdom to share with the tribe.

How can you find an elder? They are rare. First, look within your family for the people who are always asking questions. That is the elder's characteristic mode. Second, look for those to whom others look to *convene* the family. Such convening may be for a family meeting, or for the holidays, or simply for dinner. Finally, listen for the stories. As mentioned, one part of an elder's work is to tell the family's stories. If you follow the stories, you will likely find an elder.

Two Practices

Elders often fulfill their role in families in informal ways, a wise word here, a bit of encouragement there. We have also seen families build in more formal occasions for elders to practice their work. Here are two examples you may want to consider in your family.

The first is what we call a *Wisdom Council*. It forms a special part of a family governance system. (We will discuss family governance more in Chapter 20.) It institutionalizes a place within that system for nonexecutive wisdom.

For example, here is how we sometimes describe the Wisdom Council when it comes to writing up a family's governance documents:

> The Family Members who comprise the Wisdom Council are the keepers of the family's accumulated wisdom: the family's stories, its shared history, its values and its vision. They advise on matters in family disputes. Where necessary, Councilors may function as the judicial branch of the family. Their role is to listen carefully, advise a course of action, and by the nature of their stature, history, and gravitas, encourage resolution to the matter at hand. If resolution is not reached, the Wisdom Council has the authority to request outside mediation.
>
> The Family Council appoints the members of the Wisdom Council, based on those nominees' deep knowledge of the family as well as their personal wisdom and life experience. The Family Council may remove members from the Wisdom Council, if, for example, the Family Council believes that a Councilor no longer has the capacity to continue to serve in this important role.
>
> The Family Council may assign such responsibilities to the Wisdom Council as they deem appropriate, including the resolution of whether a Family Member qualifies for the role of Voting Member of the Family Assembly. In addition, the Family Council may delegate to the Wisdom Council any intra-Family dispute, including disputes between a Family Member and the Family Council or any part of the Family Enterprise, as the Family Council deems appropriate.

As you can see from these paragraphs, the Wisdom Council lives within a larger structure, overseen by the Family Council. But it looks beyond the day-to-day, month-to-month, or even year-to-year work of the rest of the family enterprise. It is focused on the family's true lineage: stories, values, and vision. It is also the ultimate defender of the family's friendship with itself. Rather than having disputes go underground, the Wisdom Council provides a trusted forum for mediating these disagreements.

The Wisdom Council cannot act on its own. It must be invited to consider a matter or act as a mediator. If no one asks, then the Wisdom Council must remain silent.

Another practice in which we have seen elders function effectively is as "trust protectors," of a sort. This is not the place to go into depth about trust protectors. Suffice it to say that a trust protector traditionally is a person or authority, named in a trust document, who often has the authority to:

- Remove or appoint trustees.
- Modify the trust for tax purposes.
- Modify beneficiaries' interests.
- Modify powers of appointment.
- Change the applicable law governing the trust.
- Terminate the trust.

As this list makes clear, a trust protector can be very powerful. It can sometimes feel as though the trust protector is a sort of super-trustee. As a result, lots of confusion can ensue.

However, what we have in mind here, as a proper role for an elder, is that of the trust protector, as champion of the trust relationships, that is, of the relationships among the grantor (the person who set up the trust), the trustee, and the beneficiary. Misunderstandings or even disputes among these three are not uncommon. How wonderful it can be, then, if a wise member of the family is empowered to serve as the mediator of this "trustscape"!

To serve as a champion, the elder should be empowered to request an annual conversation to maintain familiarity with both the trustee and the beneficiary. That conversation can revolve simply around the question, "How are things going with this trust?" In the case of a disagreement or looming conflict, the trust protector should ask each party, "What might you have done to contribute to this state of affairs?" The idea here is for the elder to use his or her special authority to encourage both parties to deepen their understanding of the situation and of each other.

Unlike the traditional trust protector, who may have the power to swoop in and make drastic changes completely of his or her own volition, we encourage designing the trust-protector-as-champion as a role that takes no further action, unless requested by the beneficiary (or possibly also by the trustee). In response to such a request, the elder could have the authority to remove and replace the trustee—or to take no action whatsoever. But, again, whatever is done would take place only after the elder had convened the trustee and beneficiary for thoughtful conversations and would be based on the elder's deep understanding of the trust and its relationships.

CHAPTER 9

Trustees and Beneficiaries

Human Consequences

Around the world, in any community shaped by English common law, trusts play a central role in many families' wealth. The reasons that family members establish trusts usually include:

- Tax minimization: putting family assets outside the reach of taxing authorities, with a view to both income taxes and to transfer taxes (i.e., estate, gift, and generation-skipping taxes).
- Asset protection: increasing the likelihood that beneficiaries' creditors or disgruntled former spouses will not be able to lay hands on family assets.
- Control: putting a representative of the founder in control of a founder-led enterprise and/or making sure that beneficiaries access family funds for the reasons, at the times, in the manner, and in the amounts that the trust creator deems best.

There is nothing inherently wrong with any of these motivations. But in years of advising trust creators fired with the dream of establishing trusts that would stand the test of generations, as well as consulting with beneficiaries who found themselves caught in the Black Hole of those dreams, we have seen some general trends:

- Generally, people find trusts to be confusing and opaque.
- The reasons for setting up trusts often ensure that by the third generation of a family's life over 90 percent of its assets have been carried into trust by a "trust wave."
- The confusing and complex nature of trusts—along with the customary silence about anything to do with money—ends up causing over 80 percent of beneficiaries to feel that their trusts are a burden, not a blessing.
- The combination of the trust wave and this feeling of burdensomeness accelerates families' entropy, dissolving their human and financial capital with great speed.

As a result, in too many cases, what starts as a way to preserve family wealth too often ends up becoming a primary source of wealth dissolution.

The factors behind this decline are emotional and relational, not legal or financial. The response must be similar. Whether you have established many trusts already, or you are considering setting up trusts for the first time, we encourage you to begin that response by considering these three questions:

1. How can your beneficiaries come to see their trusts as blessings rather than burdens?
2. How can all the people who live with your trusts make sure that these trusts embody primarily human relationships and, only afterward, legal relationships?
3. If your trustee had to terminate a trust tomorrow and distribute its assets, how could both the trustee and the beneficiary feel more secure that the beneficiary could successfully integrate those assets into his or her life?

These questions focus the attention of trustees and beneficiaries on improving the human consequences of the trust. In what follows we will summarize a few of the recommendations we offer to reach that goal.

Vocabulary

If we are going to change the way we think and act about trusts, we first need to understand how we think about them.

Our thoughts about trusts or anything else usually take the form of narratives, a collection of beliefs, assumptions, or stories. The fear of "trust-fund babies" might be part of your narrative. So, too, might be the perception that trusts equal mistrust. Alternatively, if you've had a friend whose trust helped protect his or her assets during a tough time, that would be a positive part of your narratives around trusts.

To evaluate your narratives, ask yourself these questions. What are your narratives about:

- Trusts?
- Trustees?
- Beneficiaries?
- Giving?
- Receiving?

Once you're clearer about your narratives, you can begin to change the way you speak about trusts.

To that end, ask yourself what you think a trust primarily is. Is it a document? A legal structure? A receptacle to hold assets? A tax strategy? Or a meaningful relationship?

Unsurprisingly, when we ask groups of wealth-holders this question, almost 90 percent of audience members choose one of those first four answers. Only about 10 percent say that a trust is primarily a meaningful relationship. And yet, both in law and in practice, that is what a trust is: a relationship among grantor (the person who sets up the trust), the trustee (the legal owner of the trust assets), and the beneficiary (who derives some sort of benefit from the trust assets). Documents, accounts, tax savings, and so on are all secondary to that relationship.

To highlight the relationships involved, we encourage you to think not solely of trusts but more broadly of *trustscapes*. The trustscape is the collection of relationships formed around a trust. In the simplest case, it may be limited to the grantor, trustee, and beneficiary. In many families, it may quickly encompass multiple beneficiaries, multiple trustees, trust protectors, advisers, and others (see Figure 9.1).

We recommend that trustees and beneficiaries draw a picture of the trustscape for each of their important trust relationships. It is a useful tool for remembering all the interests at play.

Second, when you create a new trust, a few points of vocabulary are crucial to set the right intention of everyone involved. For example, does the new

FIGURE 9.1 Example of a trustscape.

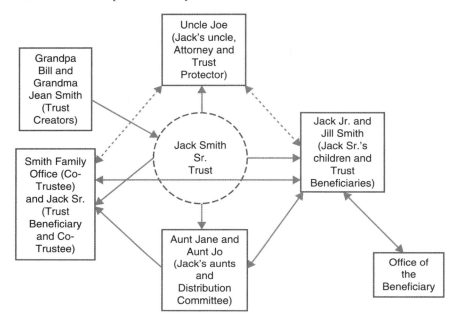

trust embody a *gift* or a *transfer*? (For more on this distinction, look back to Chapter 5.) Most trusts embody transfers.

In addition to asking whether the trust embodies a gift with spirit, if you are setting up a trust, ask yourself, "Am I a trust *creator* or a trust *signer*?" Most grantors are only trust signers. They affix their names to a document that they may not understand and that certainly does not capture their words or spirit. Trust creators, in contrast, find ways to make sure that the trust documents reflect the spirit of their gifts. These may include writing a letter of wishes to the trustee, including a preface to the trust, composing an "ethical will" to accompany the trust, or writing a personal summary or other precatory language. It may mean something as simple as thinking seriously about the name of the trust, rather than simply affixing a family name along with some legalese.

That's why one of us (Jay), for the last decade of his practice of law, would not write a trust without the grantor including some statement to the effect that:

> *This trust is a gift of love. Its purpose is to enhance the lives of the beneficiaries.*

Imagine if you were a beneficiary reading those sentences at the beginning of your trust? Would it be more likely to seem a burden or a blessing?

Many times, the only expression of purpose in a trust comes in the standards by which the trustee is to evaluate discretionary distribution requests, and those standards are often expressed in the words, "health, education, maintenance, and support." These words are used because courts have, over the years, established specific meanings to them—what's included in, say, "health" and what's not—although there are still areas of gray. (For example, is elective cosmetic surgery part of "health"? It depends.)

True trust creators can go beyond this minimal approach in a letter of wishes or letter to the trustee and beneficiaries by saying more about the trust's purposes. For example, some expressions of purpose that we have seen include:

- Productivity
  - Provide basic income for a homemaker.
  - Support a start-up.
  - Provide supplemental income for lower-paying jobs.
  - Provide income to support volunteering.
  - Support hiring a career coach.
- Education
  - Pay for tuition, housing, or meal plans.
  - Provide basic income for students.
  - Put limits on perpetual studenthood.
  - Support family unity and continuity.
  - Pay for family vacations.
  - Cover expenses for family meetings.
  - Hire facilitators or mediators.
  - Cover wedding expenses.
  - Support the adoption process.
- Legacy
  - Allow for charitable donations.
  - Pay for membership to clubs or other organizations.

We have also seen grantors compose short written statements to explain the intentions behind some of these provisions. Here are just a few examples:

Productivity

I wish for a productive adult to be considered one who, for example, holds a steady job and earns sufficient salary to provide for his or her basic needs.

I want to make sure my wealth and its disposition will not result in undermining the incentive of my heirs to lead productive lives and create other perverse incentives or outcomes.

I also view a productive adult as one in a supportive relationship who chooses to stay at home to raise children while the spouse or life partner works to provide for the family's basic needs.

Education

We see education as encompassing academic learning to advance knowledge and build a trade or career. There are many legitimate ways to be enriched outside of a classroom and we would like the funds to enable broad, lifelong learning.

Entrepreneurship

I hope that my children and other descendants will use the income and principal of the trust for the purpose of investing for profit or gain, including by investing in start-up businesses or ventures or as a source of capital for their existing business interests.

As opposed to financing a lavish lifestyle, I encourage my trustees to be liberal in distributions to enable my beneficiaries to pursue education, to purchase homes for use as primary personal residences, to pursue careers and/or to start businesses that the trustees deem to be reasonable endeavors.

Activity

Trusts succeed only if they express and encourage active—even proactive—giving and receiving. Too often, trusts fail or become stultifying because they embody inactivity that turns into reactivity.

We have shared some of the steps that a grantor can take to start to be an active giver. A good prospective trustee or adviser will encourage grantors to be active givers right from the start.

A wise trustee can be an agent for active giving and receiving at other moments in a trust's life, too. For example, the onboarding of a new beneficiary is a crucial time for encouraging activity. Such activities are part of the trustee's role as a regent or mentor. Some of the things a trustee can do to this end include:

- Reread the trust and related documents to remind yourself of its major terms.
- Write a letter or email to the new beneficiary introducing yourself, setting out a time and place for your first meeting, describing your hopes for the new relationship, offering a proposed agenda, and inviting the beneficiary to add to the agenda and to bring questions.
- Approach the new beneficiary not just with a prevention-focused mindset—that is, a focus on averting possible inappropriate requests or inquiries—but a promotion-focused mindset, that is, an attitude looking for ways that this trust—within its legal and financial limits—can enhance this beneficiary's life.
- Be mindful of the narrative that you, as a trustee, bring to this beneficiary, this family, or to beneficiaries in general. Is this narrative helpful? Or does it include generalizations or prejudices that might get in the way of a successful relationship?

If a beneficiary is to be an active recipient, that individual has some work to do, too. That work may include:

- Ask yourself, "What are my dreams? What are the activities that I feel best engaged in? What are my strengths? What are my internal hurdles? When have I worked and grown through working? If I haven't, where might I get that experience? What are the important relationships in my life? Do I feel able to advocate for myself? If not, where can I learn that skill?"
- Write a letter or email to the trustee introducing yourself, describing your hopes or aspirations, and setting out some things that you would like to talk about or learn about at your first meeting.
- Read the trust document and come to the meeting prepared with questions.
- Review your own narratives about trustees, about the grantor, and about yourself as a beneficiary. Are those narratives helpful or do they get in the way?
- Finally, cultivate a spirit of gratitude. That may be a hard step, especially if the grantor is long gone or is someone with whom you had a difficult relationship. Maybe then the gratitude focuses on some other aspect of being a member of this family, or on goods that have come from other experiences in your life. Whatever the source, expressing gratitude is an important part of completing a gift.

In sum, we share below the roles and responsibilities of beneficiaries and trustees. These are not *legal* lists. Rather, they are responsibilities that, if pursued, will make the trust a positive *human* force in the lives of everyone involved. If you are a trustee or a beneficiary, you may want to consider posting a copy of the respective list wherever you are sure to see it when reviewing your trust.

ROLES AND RESPONSIBILITIES OF BENEFICIARIES

Each beneficiary has an obligation to educate himself or herself about the duties of a beneficiary, as well as the duties of the family trustees. Here are specific responsibilities of beneficiaries.[1]

- To gain a clear comprehension of each trust in which the beneficiary has an interest and a specific understanding of the mission statement for each trust as prepared by the trustees.
- To educate himself or herself about all trustee responsibilities.
- To understand the trustee's responsibility to maintain the purchasing power of the trust's capital while maintaining a reasonable distribution rate for the income beneficiaries.
- To have a general understanding of modern portfolio theory and the formation and process of asset allocation.
- To recognize and look for proof that each trustee represents all beneficiaries.
- To meet with each trustee once each year to discuss his or her personal financial circumstances and personal goals and to advise the trustee of his or her assessment of the trustee's performance of the trustee roles and responsibilities to the trust, to the beneficiary, and to family governance.
- To become knowledgeable about the functions and importance of each element of the family's trust governance structure.
- To attend the annual family business meeting and to accept responsible roles within the family governance structure, based on his or her qualifications for such roles.
- To develop a general capacity to understand fiduciary accounting.
- To demonstrate a willingness to participate in educational sessions and to become financially literate (through family seminars and family-funded educational programs).
- To know how and in what amount trustees and other professionals are compensated and to obtain a general understanding of the budgets for the trust and investment entities in which the trust will be invested.

---

[1] We are indebted to Richard Bakal, who assisted in the development of these criteria.

ROLES AND RESPONSIBILITIES OF TRUSTEES

Each trustee has an obligation to educate himself or herself on the duties of a trustee, as well as on the duties of the trust beneficiaries.

The trustee's specific duties are as follows:

- To be fully aware of the grantor's original purposes in creating the trust and the current purposes of the trust, if these have changed over time.
- To guide his or her decisions by these purposes.
- To act so that the actual operation of the trust is empowering to the beneficiaries, within the provisions of the trust.
- To put mechanisms in place to increase the level of financial awareness of the beneficiaries, and to see that such financial education of the beneficiaries is carried out effectively.
- To meet at least annually with each beneficiary in order to renew the beneficiary's understanding of the trust, as well as to obtain from each beneficiary full information, financial and otherwise, about his or her personal situation.
- To educate himself or herself about all beneficiary responsibilities.
- To evaluate and advise each beneficiary on how well he or she is meeting the roles and responsibilities of a beneficiary.
- To implement effectively the trust's general policies and procedures as they relate to the following:
  - The trust's investment goals and acceptable risks.
  - The selection and/or provision of investment advice and management to accomplish such investment goals within the given risks.
  - The trust's tax position and the selection of tax services.
  - The trust's legal position and the selection of legal services.

Distributions

Most simply, trusts have three functions:

1. Administration: keeping track of the trust assets, taxes, notifications, and other legal requirements.
2. Investment: managing the trust assets to produce growth, income, and other aspects of a desired return.
3. Distribution: distributing trust income or principal to beneficiaries in accord with the trust's provisions.

While all three of these functions are important, the ultimate purpose of a trust is to make distributions to the beneficiary. And yet the distributive function typically lies fallow in most trusts. Trustees usually focus on administration. Grantors and even beneficiaries often pay a great deal of attention to investments. Distributions feel like an afterthought or, worse, an undesirable eventuality, to be discussed as little as possible and to be put off as long as possible. As a result, many beneficiaries find it confusing to make a discretionary distribution request. And many trustees find themselves responding to such requests in a reactive manner.

However, if there is any way by which trusts are going to become blessings rather than burdens, it is going to be through a thoughtful and proactive distribution function. This function cannot be an afterthought. It must be a primary intention from the beginning of the trust.

That's why the third question we shared at the beginning of this chapter is so helpful: "If you had to distribute the entire corpus of the trust tomorrow, would the beneficiary be ready to receive it?" Or, conversely, "If the trustee were to distribute the entire trust corpus tomorrow, would you be ready to receive it?"

To bring the distributive function to life, we propose a new model for what we call a "humane trustscape." Several forward-thinking families with whom we work are testing this model in its full form. Others have incorporated elements of it. It is not for every trust; but it does provide a goal to which specific trustscapes can aspire, based on their particularities.

To begin, we start with what, in our experience, is the model of the traditional trustscape (see Figure 9.2).

Here an institution and individual cotrustee exist in a somewhat ambiguous relationship in the middle of the field. They are clearly superior to the beneficiary, who is at the bottom of the system. But above them, perhaps, floats a mysterious trust protector, whose duties are broad but obscure, and who perhaps could swoop in at any moment to dislocate them.

In contrast to this traditional trustscape, we offer the following model (see Figure 9.3).

Here the picture is completely different. The beneficiary is at the center of the system. This by itself is a major change.

One way to put this change is to say that in the traditional model the beneficiary has neither ownership (legal title being vested in the trustee) nor control (which belongs to the trustee or perhaps the trust protector). In the humane trustscape, the family achieves what we call "control without ownership." Beneficiaries truly come into their beneficial ownership of trust assets,

FIGURE 9.2 The traditional trustscape.

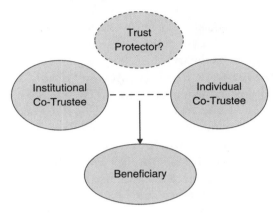

FIGURE 9.3 Model for a humane trustscape.

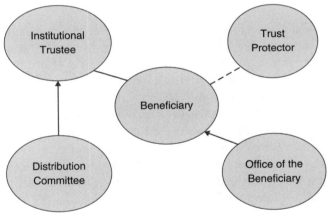

as their interests are central. At the same time, the beneficiary does not own those assets, protecting them from government sequestration or from terrible mistakes (such as an accident or a failed marriage) that could destroy the beneficiary's financial capital. This concept of control without ownership is the Holy Grail of wealth planning, yet often the forms impede this function.

Key to giving the beneficiary some sense of control is the body we call the Distribution Committee or DC. The DC may be a committee or one person. Its sole function is to advise the trustee about distributions. In pursuit of that end, it must get to know the beneficiary and understand what kinds of beneficiaries could be helpful to that individual's flourishing. The DC then goes back to the trustee with that knowledge. It advises; it does not distribute. As a result, it is not a fiduciary. The DC works for the trustee and is paid from the trust. The trustee can change the DC at any time, though the function will likely exist so long as the trust is making distributions.

On the other side is the Beneficiary Advisory Board (BAB). As with the DC, this could be an individual or a group. The difference is that the BAB serves the beneficiary alone. Its function is to help the beneficiary ensure that he or she can integrate the trust and its distributions effectively into his or her life. This work may take the form of helping the beneficiary learn about the trust or about finances. It may take the form of mentoring the beneficiary about work, relationships, or communication. For these different forms, the BAB may draw on different individuals: family members, friends, advisers, or family office staff. But the BAB serves the beneficiary. The beneficiary decides when and to what degree the BAB functions. Ideally, the beneficiary should also pay for the BAB, either out of pocket or from distributions for his or her benefit.

Our model also includes a trust protector. But this protector is not the nebulous, "super-trustee" of most traditional trustscapes. Instead, as mentioned in Chapter 8, we recommend renaming the protector the "trust champion," and using the trust champion in a solely mediative function. The champion will have only one task: to mediate disputes between beneficiary and trustee. To achieve this goal the champion will need to talk at least annually with the beneficiary and the trustee, to check on the health of the relationship. But the champion will become active only upon the request of the beneficiary (or possibly upon the request of either the beneficiary or the trustee). In such a case, the champion will try to convene a discussion of the situation and mediate a result. In the case of an impasse, the champion has the power to remove the trustee and appoint a new one—or to do nothing. Because the champion has no purview over distributions, it would not be a fiduciary. As a result, this role might be the perfect one for family elders, friends, or trusted advisers who otherwise would not or could not serve as a trustee.

Finally, there is the trustee. We suggest an institutional trustee because in this model the trustee's main function will be to maintain strong administration, oversee the investing, and establish and heed the advice of the Distribution Committee. Institutions with a track record for fidelity are well-positioned to serve in this role, as a sort of backbone to the system, while integrating the wisdom of the rest of the parts.

Conclusion

If there is anything that our collective decades living with family trusts has taught us, it is humility. Though simple in concept, the task of living well among trusts is amazingly complex. Our hope is that by focusing attention on the human side of trust relationships, we will be able to achieve the goal of increasing the number of such relationships that are blessings rather than burdens, and that truly embody the best part of grantors' dreams to enhance the lives of family members for years to come.

Because navigating trusts is such a complex and specialized topic, many families invite their beneficiaries and trustees to pursue dedicated learning on this topic. If your family is interested in such learning, please see Appendix One, where we have reproduced the agenda for a multi-day "Fiduciary Course Curriculum."

CHAPTER 10

Advisers

You can define a straight line; what use is that to you if you've no idea what straightness means in life?

Seneca, writing about "experts"

Questions to Consider

Family wealth is a "high-credence" field. That means that it is not always clear to people using services how results are achieved and how performance is or should be measured. If a dentist does something wrong, you feel it. A wealth adviser's advice may appear mistaken only long after the fact. As a result, most clients engage with advisers, at least in part, on trust. That's why personal charm, friendly recommendations, and prestige often complement or even replace cold analysis in the selection of advisers.

When meeting with a prospective new adviser or reviewing an established adviser's work, we find a set of questions helpful to guide the discussion. These include the following:

- What specific services will I receive (or have I been receiving)?
- Who will work with my family, and in what capacity?
- How do you differ from other advisers in this space?

What Specific Services Will I Receive (or Have I Been Receiving)?

The first question gets at the crucial matter of what services you can expect from the adviser. Over time, families may come to enjoy personal rapport and closeness with their advisers. But the foundation of any rapport must be tangible services from the adviser to the client, and most of these services in wealth advising take expertise and time to provide.

Who Will Work with My Family, and in What Capacity?

This question gets at the adviser's service model. Most financial advisers work in teams. The team approach can help clients get specialized advice fast and in an integrated manner. It can also make it hard to understand who does what.

How Do You Differ from Other Advisers in This Space?

This question identifies what the adviser considers the qualities that distinguish them from others. Advisers will often point to what they consider their strengths, whether in investments or planning or family dynamics. Once they do so, it is important to ask for tangible examples of how they deliver.

Money

Advice does not come free. Part of your task as a client is to evaluate the price for that advice versus its value.

To approach this comparison of price and value, here are some questions that you can ask your own advisers or prospective advisers:

- Since your practice must grow to flourish, what percentage of your time do you spend on seeking new clients?
- What percentage of your time do you spend directly on work with and for your own clients?
- How many clients do you have final responsibility for?

There are no hard and fast percentages to look for in those first two questions. They will often depend on where the adviser is in his or her practice development. Advisers just starting a business will naturally spend more time on marketing. That is why it is helpful also to know how many clients an adviser has final responsibility for serving. Fewer does not simply mean better and more does not automatically mean worse. It all depends on what you as the client are seeking.

It is also important to ask an adviser, "What are the various ways that you get paid?" Since revenue incentivizes behavior, it is natural for advisers to recommend products or services that make them money.

It is hard to talk about money with anyone, including advisers. That said, it is good practice to discuss fees with your adviser at least once a year and to take the lead in that conversation. There are a few principles and practices that can help you make that conversation productive:

- Make sure fee proposals are clear and written.
- Ask your adviser to put his or her fees in context.
- Watch how your adviser responds to questions about the fees. How your advisers respond to these questions or this conversation could serve as a sign of their competence, experience, and good intent.

A fair fee and a good fee discussion can bring the adviser's good and the client's good into congruence, and, rather than driving people apart, it can provide the foundation for a productive relationship.

Personnes de Confiance

All these points also apply to the special class of advisers who help families grow their complete family wealth. These advisers we call *personnes de confiance*. It is hard to categorize them by a single profession or field, although they may have started out as a lawyer, accountant, financial adviser, or psychologist. Sometimes, though, a *personne de confiance* may appear in the guise of a friend, a teacher, a priest, an intellectual, an in-law, or a manager.

As diverse as they may appear, *personnes de confiance* do share qualities in common:

- An interest in culture: A true number two recognizes that no family leader, no matter how forceful, can by himself or herself effect lasting change. A system, such as a family, requires agreement and engagement to carry out a visionary's vision.
- A belief in orderly evolutionary change: Sometimes visible change happens quickly. But it is always almost preceded by unseen, gradual adjustments. Beware of an adviser who promises to change your family culture in the space of a single meeting.

- Subordination of ambition to a higher calling: A number two is, by definition, not number one. Some people recoil at the thought of such subordination. But we have seen numerous cases when the quiet efforts of a true number two have had more positive effects on a family's long-term flourishing than the more noticeable actions of hyperactive number ones.

Personne de confiance is a high-sounding title. In essence, what we are describing here is someone who puts your family—the whole family—first, in terms of preserving and growing all the family's capital. The role is defined by attitude, not skills. Ask yourself: Is there someone in your network of advisers who takes that perspective? If so, hold tight to him or her. If not, start looking for someone who does.

Counselors, Coaches, and Facilitators

One type of *personne de confiance* who can play a large role in the journey of family wealth is the counselor, facilitator, or coach. Such counselors may advise individuals around life or career, or work with the entire family, say, in preparing for a family meeting or a discussion of governance. Many counselors and coaches are well-trained and effective. Some are not. Because there are no generally accepted standards for this role, if you are considering engaging a counselor or facilitator, here are some questions to ask yourself:

- What are the aspects of your life, individually or as a family, that you would like to improve?
- Do these areas of concern have more to do with your career or more to do with your heart?
- Are you willing to make time to meet regularly and to reflect on your meetings?
- Are you willing to be honest and authentic with someone else about parts of yourself or your family relationships that you may not like?

If the answers to these questions have led you to conclude that you are ready for a counseling relationship, then here are some questions or criteria to consider in seeking out a suitable coach or counselor:

- What is the prospective counselor's training?
- Does the prospective counselor have a medically accepted license?

- What is the prospective counselor's experience? In work? In counseling?
- Does that experience line up with the challenges you are seeking to work on?

Entering a counseling relationship always involves some element of trust, and it is a two-way street. But it does not have to be a pure leap of faith. Consider meeting two times, first, with any prospective counselor or coach, to assess each other and your possible relationship. If, after two meetings, you both agree that there is a productive fit, then you can proceed to more regular sessions. If not, then neither you nor the counselor has invested a significant amount of time or money in a relationship that would probably not work anyway. These initial two meetings also give you and the counselor some time to explore the possible goals for your work together. Even if you do not keep meeting after that, the work you do in these two sessions may prove useful to you as you continue your journey.

Mentors

There is one more type of adviser or *personne de confiance* that we want to touch upon: the mentor. Most mentors today focus their efforts on a task or process of adjustment. A mentor may help you at school or at a new job or at various times in your career. But a true mentor does more than help you *adjust*. A true mentor helps you *evolve*.

A true mentor is rare. What are a mentor's characteristics? First, a mentor is experienced. Most often, this experience accompanies old age, but it may be won earlier in life. Second, a mentor is trusted. It takes time and familiarity for someone to become a mentor. Third, as mentioned, a mentor does not focus just on one task or adjustment. Finally, being a mentor takes some wit or even guile. Authenticity is all well and good. But a mentee may not always be ready for the truth. A mentor must know how much to reveal and when. This last point means that you may meet a mentor—or perhaps have already met a mentor—and not quite know it at the time.

Mentorship is not a relationship that can be forced or demanded. After all, Athena, the original mentor, was a goddess. She came and went as she wished. Perhaps the best thing that you can do is to open your heart to the possibility of mentorship. In our experience, when the heart is ready, the mentor appears.

A Father's Wisdom

We end this chapter on advisers with a few words of wisdom from one of Jay's mentors, his father James Elliott Hughes Sr., himself a model counselor and adviser:

Eighty percent of the time, do nothing.

Sometimes the best resolution for a matter is time. Delaying action may be one of the most valuable actions an adviser can take vis-à-vis his or her clients. James Sr. made the same point, "Obey the Law of Tardy" and "Hasten slowly."

The beginning of anything is often farther down the road than we perceive.

Because we are often focused on the present moment and all that's led up to it, we believe that we are either at the beginning or a long way down the road. In fact, the true beginning of any important endeavor—including the journey of complete family wealth—usually becomes clear only after many hours and many false starts.

Think in long-term ways; use history to understand.

This is especially important advice for families. Every family combines memories of people who lived generations ago with people who will make an impact three generations or more into the future. A focus on today or this quarter or this year cannot meet the challenges families face.

Take small steps and succeed together before trying to tackle the most difficult problems.

Often families want to take on the big problems right away. Advisers who encourage this tendency may shine for a moment, but usually those big problems are difficult for a reason. It takes time to understand, much less change, a family's culture. Only success built on success has a chance of doing so.

Bring those who are complaining inside the group and give them important roles to play.

Most families and their advisers relegate complainers to the periphery, where they happily keep up their sniping. As a result, nothing really changes. Bringing complainers into the group can have the result of mitigating their discontent. It may also put valid complaints on the table and contribute to long-term positive change.

CHAPTER 11

Friends

One of the great challenges for individuals with wealth is the question, "Do my friends like me for who I am or for what I have?" We hope the following section sparks some thinking about what a true friend is for you.

Friends as Wealth

According to his student Xenophon, the philosopher Socrates once spoke about friends this way:

> Many people know the number of their other possessions, even when they have many things. But of their friends, even if they have just a few, not only are they ignorant of the number, but also to those who ask them to list their friends they set down some and then again take them out. Such is their mindfulness about their friends![1]

Think about this point for a moment. How many houses do you have? How many bank accounts? How much money in each account? Now think about your friends. How many would you list? Do some names shuttle on and off the list? What is different about asking yourself about your houses or bank accounts versus your friends?

---

[1] Xenophon, *Memorabilia of Socrates* (London: Cassell, 2014), II.4.4.

If you reflect on these questions, you will agree that the challenge Socrates poses is not one limited to fifth-century BC Athens. The difficulty of listing our friends seems an enduring one.

And yet pretty much everyone's idea of living well includes spending time with friends and loved ones. These may be family members, spouses or partners, boyfriends, girlfriends, work friends, school friends, and friendly acquaintances that are more casual but still add charm to life. A life without friends would seem miserable, even inhuman.

Why, then, is it so much more difficult to catalog our friends than our financial capital?

Part of the challenge seems to be that friends do not stay put the way that houses or other possessions do. Friendships are often changing. One person may be a new acquaintance who is on his or her way to becoming a friend. Another person may be drifting away, on his or her way to becoming a former friend. The lines between prospective friend, friend, and former friend seem fuzzy.

Most people also have different types of friends. You might have a best friend or even a couple of best friends. You probably have close friends versus friendly acquaintances. You may have friends specific to a context, such as school, work, or family. Some people may feel like close friends and yet see each other only once or twice a year. You might not place them on a list of friends unless you are thinking about a specific context.

Aristotle speaks of three types of friends.[2] First are friends of utility. We might call these "friendly acquaintances." Such a friendship aims at getting a job done. It is the kind of relation you might have with your banker, landscaper, or a clerk at a store. Second are friends of pleasure. These are people we enjoy spending time with, at dinners, parties, or entertainment. They are fun, and life needs some fun. Third are what Aristotle calls friends of virtue. These friends are rare. Such friends encourage each other to be as excellent as possible—in whatever area of life matters to them most. They truly delight in each other's success.

Try cataloging your friendships this way: Who are your most important friends of utility? Who are your friends of pleasure? Who are your friends of virtue?

---

[2] Aristotle, *The Nicomachean Ethics* (London: Penguin, 2003), Book Eight.

These complexities—the changes in friendships and the different types of friendships—all point to a more fundamental question: What is a friend? This is not a type of question one faces with respect to houses, cars, dogs or cats, stocks or bonds. The difficulty of cataloging our friends may derive, at least in part, from the difficulty of answering this fundamental question.

The question is difficult because there is something precious and delicate about friendship. It wants protection and care. But maybe, at bottom, the delicacy of friendship comes down to what *we* want of it. Don't we each want our friends to love us for who we are—to care about us and, when push comes to shove, to put us first? "A friend in need is a friend indeed." To that end, we hope to be deserving of our friends' care and sacrifice. And yet cataloging our friends threatens to take away the veil from this delicate dance of hope. Socrates likens our friends to our other possessions. Possessions are things that we make use of, for our own benefit. If we look at our friends as possessions, from which we hope to benefit, do we deserve their care?

Wealth and Friends

If we think through what we are truly looking for in friendship, we will be in a much better position to be good friends ourselves. This is the key to friendship generally.

Great financial capital brings added complexity to friendship. As mentioned, many members of the rising generation in families with significant wealth worry that friends do not like them for who they are but rather for what they have. This worry can be exacerbated when their family name is publicly known or when their parents or grandparents have made significant gifts to their schools or colleges. We have even known of situations where teachers have called out rising-generation family members in their classrooms, commenting on their parents' financial capital.

Again, the key to having good friends is being a good friend. When it comes to dealing with friends, roommates, or the like about money, some of the more specific practices that we have found helpful include:

- *Creative omission*: If it's not already known, it's not necessary to draw attention to your financial resources. As we mentioned in the early part of this book, there are times when the old taboo on talking about money is quite healthy.

- *Deflecting the conversation away from others' speculation about what you have*: Be ready with other topics for conversation. Most people will get the hint.
- *Redirecting the conversation back to what's important*: What your goals are, what you're trying to achieve, and how these choices will impact your relationship as friends.
- *Proper assertiveness*: If someone is not getting the hint and it's not appropriate to talk about money, then say so. "My family's resources are something we treat as private, and my family members rely on me to uphold that value. As my friend, I hope you understand that."

Because these situations arise so pervasively at school or college, we recommend that every family with a large number of rising-generation members who are teenagers to 20-somethings make time at family meetings to talk about these challenges. Support each other as a group. Learn from what older cousins or older-generation family members have experienced. We have heard family members productively discuss everything from how best to split a dinner bill to how to make decisions about where to go on Spring Break with friends with fewer resources. You do not need to navigate these added complexities of friendship amid financial wealth alone.

Most importantly, do not feel guilty. If you are a good friend, then you will have plenty of things—and more important things—to contribute to your friendships beyond money.

PART THREE

CHAPTER 12

Character

History

In the field of family wealth over the past few decades, much effort has focused on developing and promulgating the vocabulary we are sharing in these pages. This vocabulary responds directly to many families' anxiety that their riches will ruin their descendants' lives and so leave future family members both financially and spiritually impoverished.

This anxiety is perennial, as suggested by the persistence (even in the face of contrary empirical evidence) of the proverb "shirtsleeves to shirtsleeves in three generations." And yet, our vocabulary is new.

What did families do before these new ideas came along? They certainly had advisers, but those advisers—brokers, accountants, and tax attorneys—mainly tended the family's financial riches. From their ranks, occasional *personnes de confiance* appeared, but usually only in families with significant political or business interests. The *personne de confiance* might discreetly fix a delicate personal or business affair and then quietly return to his professional duties.

If we peer back into the past, from, say, the early nineteenth century through the 1950s, we find that the two most authoritative guides of wealthy families' nonfinancial affairs were not advisers but rather custom and law. Some of these customs included well-defined practices for children's education (understood not just as schooling but also as education of the whole person), including sport, roughing it, and service in business, charity, and the military. Others included strong opinions about the work and behavior expected of wealthy men and women, inside and outside the home. The most supportive laws were those around trusts and estates, which established allegiance to fiduciary rules in many families, an attitude captured by the word "stewardship." As a result, many families who combined sound financial and legal advice with respect for these laws and customs slowed and even at times reversed family wealth's natural entropy.

In some families, these laws and customs also led to the adoption of specific governance structures. They certainly influenced how families made decisions. But these structures or ways of decision-making were not the whole story. What law and custom truly shape is character, the character of individuals and of families. Shaped by law and custom, it was character that allowed families in the past to succeed—when they did succeed—at long-term wealth preservation.

Why then has the new vocabulary become necessary? The social revolution of the 1960s, together with the financial devastation of the 1970s, largely put an end to the old ways. Past norms of education and behavior were dismissed as oppressive, unproductive, or obsolete. The old upper class, with shared norms about work, charity, and spending, largely faded away. A new upper class, marked out more by credentials than by pedigree, took its place. Fiduciary rules came to seem a legal game, meant only to reduce taxes. The continual rewriting of these rules by Congress since 1976 has only confirmed this attitude.

As a result, we live in unsettled times. Since the 1980s, affluence has increased. So, too, has the freedom of the wealthy. But this affluence and freedom are double-edged swords. Concerns about wealth's impact once felt by a few hundred families are now shared by millions. And long gone are the social forces that shaped the character that helped the few deal with those concerns. There are many more wealthy families than in the past, but each family feels left to its own devices, having to invent a system to keep itself together.

These changes bring us to the present. It is the decline in the force of the old customs that has made necessary the new words and the new ways they describe. This vocabulary gains added force from the fact that the new generations that currently control much of the financial capital in the world are much more comfortable with psychological language and approaches than their forebears.

Character has fallen into the shadows.

That doesn't mean that the new approach doesn't have its virtues. It has reminded families what past families always knew: the real danger to family wealth is from families themselves. Further, it has given families a course of action. That course may include establishing deliberative and educational bodies within the family, conversing about questions that really matter, or committing to working as a family, combining members' views in a mission statement, and giving members opportunities to learn and demonstrate skills needed for family unity.

What Works

We have seen this new approach effect positive change in families. But perhaps not for the reasons some family members or advisers believe. The key, we believe, is *not* simply the vocabulary or the practices, as important as they are. Rather, this vocabulary and these practices reconnect families with the core concept of character. So, if we want to continue to improve our families, it is crucial that we understand and engage consciously and directly with character.

Common sense confirms that practices such as communicating, deciding how to decide, and helping family members learn will contribute to well-being.

But are such practices the whole story? Are they even the most important part of the story? Rather, it may be that these practices are just the tip of a much larger iceberg. Perhaps, in many cases, these practices or structures work because they are embedded in more complex family *enterprises*, which often have well-defined characters. In other cases, they may get their effectiveness from their conjunction with other family traditions or beliefs—such as religious faith—that may have little to do with governance.

In short, when one finds success, one may find good governance, but that doesn't mean that such governance causes the success. Rather, it may be that where one finds success, one finds character, which itself gives rise *both* to certain forms of governance *and* to long-term success. This is a conclusion that many family leaders feel in their heart; they just sometimes find it hard to express in words and act on it.

If it is true, if character is the key, then it leads to important consequences for the work of growing family wealth over time.

One of the most daunting consequences concerns time. Long-term success may depend mainly on the slow development of family character. That slowness may require that families take care not to let the growth of their financial capital outstrip the growth of their human qualities. That's a problem for families who experience the arrival of sudden money. Further, the growth of character is not the work of a quarter or even a year but rather of decades, even generations. Are most families—not to mention most advisers—ready to commit themselves to such a time frame?

We began with referring to one proverb. We will end with another:

If you are planning for the year, plant rice.
If you are planning for the decade, plant trees.
If you are planning for the centuries, grow men and women.

Growing men and women means focusing on character.

CHAPTER 13

Work

Meaning

If we are to take character seriously, as we suggested in Chapter 12, then most people would say, "Get to work." Work seems tightly connected to the development of character.

That is why we touched on the importance of work in Chapter 4, on the Rising Generation. Here we want to expand those comments to situate work within the development of character, for individuals and for a family.

Many people today say that work should aim at "meaning." Our goal should be to do meaningful work. Meaning might sound like a luxury. If you don't have to work to make ends meet or feed and clothe your children, then you can indulge in pursuing meaning.

But, to the contrary, some say that even menial work can be meaningful if pursued in the right way. Meaning sounds like it is a candidate for defining good work, from the bottom of the economic spectrum to the top. It would also define good work, whether that work is paid or unpaid. Charitable efforts can be as meaningful as running a commercial empire. So, too, can be the work of parenting young children or caring for elderly parents.

Think for a moment about yourself:

- What would you say is your work? It might be something different than your job or your title.
- Do you find meaning in your work? If so, how would you describe that meaning?

If meaning is the thread that runs through all true work, what is meant by meaning? Contemporary psychologists are debating this very question. For positive psychology, meaning is a key term, describing the devotion of "your signature strengths and virtues in the service of something much larger than you are."[1] Meaning comes from not acting solely for oneself or one's own good. It is the sense that there is a whole larger than oneself, perhaps even a sort of common good, to which one's efforts contribute. Perhaps that contribution is large. Perhaps it is small. Whatever its size, if it is in the service of something larger, it is meaningful.

Meaning also addresses our common fate. Time casts down both the great and the small. In contrast, meaning seems to offer hope: hope that each of us can contribute to something larger, something better, something that will outlive our efforts.

Strengths and Flow

How then can we foster meaningful work?

As mentioned, according to positive psychology, meaningful work involves serving something larger than yourself through the application of your signature strengths and virtues. So doing meaningful work requires identifying your signature strengths and virtues.

Reflecting on your past experiences is a simple way to begin to identify your strengths. Consider these questions:

- When do you feel that you have done your best work? Again, this might not be a specific job or even paid work.
- What characterized this work?
- What was it about you, the work, or the conditions of the work that contributed to it going so well?

When you reflect on these questions about your work experiences, what are some of the words that come to mind describing yourself? What are the positive qualities, strengths, or virtues that you applied in doing this good work?

---

[1] Martin E.P. Seligman, *Authentic Happiness* (New York: Free Press, 2002), 263.

The Human Work

All our various jobs, careers, practices, or arts aim at specific goods. Doctors aim at health, architects at designing beautiful and useful buildings, and engineers at building them safely. But is there some good that encompasses all the others, and at which these other, partial goods aim? If there is, perhaps that encompassing good would be found not in the work of this or that craftsman but in the work of the human being as such. It would seem odd to say that each of us, as a worker, has specific work to do, but as human beings we are pointless.

What would the specifically human work look like? The philosopher Aristotle observed that we share living—eating, growing, and so forth—with all other living things. Even feelings we share with animals such as dogs and cats. What seems peculiar to human beings—at least until we find other such beings among the stars—is the exercise of reason. So Aristotle concludes his initial thoughts on our work with this long sentence:

> So if the work of the human being is an activity according to reason or not without reason, and we say that this same work belongs to the individual and the serious individual (just as the same work belongs to a lyre-player and a serious lyre-player) with the addition of the excess in excellence added to the work (for a lyre-player plays the lyre, but a serious one plays it well), and if this is so, and if we posit that the work of the human being is a certain way of life, and we posit that this way of life is an activity of the soul and actions done with reason, and it belongs to the serious man to do these well and beautifully, and each thing is completed well in accord with its proper excellence, and if this is so, the human good comes to be an activity of the soul in accordance with excellence, and if there are several excellences, in accord with the best and most complete.[2]

This is heavy going. And it is thoroughly conditional: notice all those "ifs." But it is precisely if we take our day-to-day work seriously that, Aristotle says, we must wonder about our all-encompassing work. His long sentence is not a dogmatic end to our thinking but an invitation to pursue it.

---

[2] Aristotle, *The Nicomachean Ethics* (London: Penguin, 2003), I.7.14–15.

Play

We cannot do justice to Aristotle's invitation here. Instead, we'll offer one observation. The example that he uses most prominently to illuminate the human work is the activity of a lyre player. No doubt there are many reasons for this choice. Music seems to animate the soul while also making use of the body. It depends on number and proportion but it speaks to the passions. It can involve speech but it does not rely on speech. Despite Aristotle's emphasis on reason, his example subtly reminds us that we are not brains in a vat.

The lyre player also reminds us that life is not all work. Lyre playing is just that: a sort of play. Part of the appeal of music is that it frees us, at least for a moment, from our day-to-day concerns and struggles. It can dissolve our seriousness and our habits of drudgery. "In music the passions enjoy themselves," as the German philosopher Nietzsche wrote.[3]

Indeed, Johan Huizinga argues that all elements of culture—from children's games, to education, to music, art, philosophy, business, and even politics—find their core element in play.[4] Play creates a sacred space, that rejuvenates us by taking us away from the mundane, the worldly, the average, or the workaday. Huizinga ironically hypothesizes that play might just be the most serious thing in human life.

Consider your own time apart from work:

- What do you do with your time apart from work?
- How do you describe this time? Is it downtime? Or up? Do you look forward to it or avoid it?
- What would you imagine doing if you were to spend all your time not working?

With the example of the lyre player and Huizinga's speculations in mind, could we say that Aristotle is suggesting that our most serious work is a sort of play? This is a challenging question for a world in which most of us think that work is the most serious thing and that play is mere entertainment. It requires recapturing a forgotten wisdom that holds that relaxation (resting,

---

[3] Friedrich Nietzsche, *Beyond Good and Evil* (1886), aphorism 106.
[4] See Johan Huizinga, *Homo Ludens: A Study of the Play-Element of Culture* (Boston: Beacon Press, 1955).

sleeping, entertainment) is for the sake of work—to recharge us to continue our efforts—while work itself is for the sake of something higher.[5]

What is work for? Is there an endless series of ends, each one pointing to something beyond itself, but with the whole series being pointless? Or is there some activity that is sufficient to itself? Music, again, seems to shine as an example. Yes, one can play music for a paycheck or for fame or for some other external goal. But in its simplest and purest form, music delights us for its own sake.

We cannot face the facets of these questions without thinking through for ourselves the fundamental issues: Can I find fulfillment in an activity that is neither work nor preparation for work? Can I find a form of play that is not mere relaxation? Is there anything I do that is simply "for its own sake"? What would it mean to me for such play to be the pinnacle of my living well? Could it be that the most complete meaning comes to us not when we are working on or in the world but when we are still, quiet, and listening to what is?

Along these lines, we will give the last word here not to Aristotle but to his predecessor, Pythagoras, who was an early philosopher-mystic. Pythagoras offered the following comparison:

> Life is like the Olympic Games. In the arena are the contestants, striving to win. Around them are the spectators, cheering or booing. And wandering through the stands are the vendors, selling drinks and snacks and the like. These three types of people represent the three main ways of life. There is the life of those who seek honor: the gold medal, the cheers of the crowd, deathless fame. There is the life of those who want money, buying and selling wares. And then there is the life of the spectator, who finds pleasure in watching the contestants, his fellow spectators, and this entire game called life.

Who are you now in the stadium of life—a contestant, a vendor, or a spectator? Who do you want to be, and why?

---

[5] On this point, see Josef Pieper, *Leisure, the Basis of Culture*, trans. Gerald Malsbury (South Bend, IN: St. Augustine's Press, 1998).

CHAPTER 14

Talking with Children about Wealth

Development

As with other important life skills, learning about money and wealth is developmental. It is crucial to adapt the lesson to the appropriate developmental stage of the child or young adult who is doing the learning.

We find this simple chart helpful in breaking down the complex topic of teaching children about wealth.

Age range	Message/Activity
5–8	"We have more than enough."
9–12	Encouragement of industry—allowances
13–18	Basic financial skills and knowledge
18–21	Managing independence
21–25	Introduction to structures, their purposes, and eventually assets
25+	Engagement in family enterprise governance: "interdependence"

In what follows, we will focus on the first four stages: from early childhood through late adolescence. Chapter 4 discusses skills and practices appropriate to when members of the rising generation are starting to find their own way through life.

The Power of the Teachable Moment

Like learning to read, financial literacy is a long-term process that best starts in early childhood. We cannot assume our children will learn good money attitudes and skills unless we take the time to teach them.

A key to raising responsible children amid wealth is finding or creating teachable moments in everyday life when money lessons can be learned. People may think that wealth brings more of these moments than does middle-class life. Unfortunately, the opposite is true. As the French philosopher Rousseau put it, wealth may deprive children of a "natural education."

For example, one of us once took his daughter, then 7 years old, to her first book fair at her private school. The school wanted to make buying books easy for the parents and for the school, so beforehand the school had asked the father for his credit card number and a limit, say, $30, for the daughter's purchases. The 7-year-old navigated the fair, picked out several books she liked, and took them to the register. The salesperson entered some figures on a laptop and gave the books back to the girl, who then turned to her dad and proudly said, "Buying books is easy!"

Clearly, dad had missed a chance to introduce useful money skills: to show his daughter what $30 looks like, to have her handle the bills, to figure out that three $9 books cost $27, to watch the salesperson add on tax and make change, and to connect an upper limit—$30—with the inability to buy a fourth or fifth book.

Young children learn about money as a tangible thing—holding it, counting it, putting it in piggy banks, giving it away, and sometimes losing it. Mastering basic skills with cash lays the groundwork for later being able to make the transition safely to more abstract money transactions using digital currencies, wireless payments, credit cards, ATMs, and checks.

Are We Rich?

Up to age 8 or so, children's main developmental needs are love, attachment, and a sense of security. That is why it is not unusual for children to ask their parents at some point, "Are we rich?"

Even the best-prepared parents can freeze in their tracks at this question. If handled well, it offers a significant teachable moment.

First, recognize that when it comes from young children, this question is not about money. Your 6-year-old is not angling to know your estate plan.

This question simply reflects a desire for comfort and security, perhaps piqued by comparisons with friends' or other relatives' houses.

Try drawing out your child as to what's prompting the question, but don't respond with suspicion or concern: "Why do you ask?" or "Who told you that?" An interrogation will only breed worry and shut down future discussion.

Nor does it help to lie or dodge the question: "Oh, we're not rich. The so-and-sos are 10 times richer!" This comparison will make your child feel insecure or jealous, and eventually your child will learn you evaded the truth.

Instead, we recommend that you accept this question as an opening to introduce these simple distinctions: *not enough, enough,* and *more than enough.*

"Many families," you can point out, "do not have enough. Some have just enough, and others have more than enough. We are very fortunate to have more than enough. That's why we can have many good things, and why we often share some of what we have with families who don't have enough." In this brief comment, you let your child know that he or she is secure and you also present your family as caring about others.

Curiosity

The middle years of childhood are especially important for their role in money skills development. The period from ages 9 through 12 is the best time for training about money. This is when children can learn not only the fundamentals of how money works but also a sense of initiative to propel them through life.

Children in this preadolescent stage are often very interested in learning about money. They will enjoy being shown how to calculate tips in a restaurant, how quickly they can estimate 25 percent off in a sale, or how to compare the value of two sizes of foods. These examples may seem trivial. But you must look at the world from the child's point of view. Focus on things the child is interested in and can learn from. Research shows these early experiences lay the groundwork for later self-responsibility, good money values, and a critical eye for what things are worth.

Allowances

Allowances rub some families the wrong way. Some parents grew up in tough circumstances without allowances, forcing them to earn money from an early age. Or they bridle at the notion of giving their kids a handout or a salary for chores. We have often heard parents say, "My kids should do chores because they're part of this family, not for money."

We do not recommend treating allowances as a gift, a salary, a reward for grades, or an entitlement. Handouts are easy but they don't help children learn. An allowance can still be very useful. An allowance is a constant source of teachable moments, giving you as a parent a way to foster your child's financial training. Approaching an allowance this way shifts the focus from what the child has done to *get* the money to what the child plans to *do* with the money.

For example, many families ask their children to allocate their allowance to three buckets: one-third for present spending, one-third for savings, and one-third for giving away charitably. This system teaches many lessons at once. It underscores that the family's values include not only spending but also saving and philanthropy. By devoting a portion to savings, children learn about delayed gratification and long-term planning. And it provides a vehicle for children to practice making their own decisions about money safely, learning from both successes and setbacks.

If an allowance is to provide these benefits, then you should try not to micromanage your child's choices around spending. You may cringe at times at spending decisions he or she may make, but remember: the goal is to teach, not to control. That's how children learn. You can exercise a "no" if the expenditure would violate the family's shared sense of what's right and wrong. Finally, don't revoke an allowance as punishment. This just teaches that you will use money to show anger.

The real power of an allowance is in its ability to teach by experience. If your 12-year-old knows his or her allowance must last all month yet spends it all on clothes in the first week, then he or she must either do without or earn more money for the rest of the month. It's a lesson few children forget. The key here is not to jump in and bail your children out. The message of a bailout is: "Don't worry: there are no consequences for what you do." This is exactly the opposite of what you want to teach.

Delay of gratification is one of the greatest teachers. By having some rules around spending—and not bailing your children out when they veer from the path—you will help them learn.

Adolescents

The teenage years (ages 13–18) pose special challenges for financial parenting, particularly if you've let those earlier opportunities slide by. Your kids may turn into people you barely recognize, making increasingly risky decisions even they may regret later. Teachable moments evaporate as peers and the media take over as major influences.

Here again, the institutions of wealth can deny your children potential opportunities for learning financial skills. For example, a family office can too easily cross the line from helping to removing responsibility from teenagers needing to learn financial discipline.

How to foster your teenager's financial literacy? There are at least three main areas:

1. *Information.* Use the advertising that bombards your teenagers as teachable moments about interest rates. Talk about compound interest. Demonstrate online investment tracking. Explain how to read monthly statements, starting with a smaller account that may already be in the child's name. Teach your child how to write checks and balance a checkbook, even if these responsibilities can be delegated later in life.
2. *Values.* In retelling the family history of how the wealth was created, emphasize the work and risk that were undertaken, not to instill guilt but to teach that work and risk are fundamentals of success. As purchases get more expensive (cars, travel, parties), make your teen subsidize more of their cost. This demonstrates that the family hands over greater responsibility as the next generation matures.
3. *Decision-making.* Teenagers can be natural-born debaters, not always to their benefit. Foster healthy decision-making by prompting your teenagers to make their case responsibly when they want something new, whether a BMW or a trip to Italy. This should not be an exercise in glib argument. Have them truly explain the reasoning behind requests, showing they've looked at costs, benefits, and alternatives. Stay open but firm. They will gradually learn how to think carefully about choices. You will be rewarded when they are able to drop an extravagant request after they've truly explored things. Of course, sometimes a purchase goes against deeply held family values. Then it's time to say no, with an explanation. This way, you teach the crucial lesson that life doesn't fulfill every wish, even for children in families with wealth.

Managing teenagers and cars deserves a book in its own right. With relation to family wealth, adolescents' interest in driving can lead to a series of teachable moments. The key here, again, is to set clear expectations. Just because you can buy a 16-year-old a new luxury vehicle doesn't mean that a 16-year-old should expect such a car. Many families we know set the expectation that new drivers will drive used cars—and help pay for, say, half the cost of purchasing the vehicle, in addition to gas. If the eager young driver does not work or save for gas money, then the car sits in the driveway. We have known many teenagers who took considerable pride in earning money to pay for Toyotas, Hondas, or Lexuses only a few years younger than they are.

All these strategies assume one thing: time together. You can't discuss information, values, or decisions if you and your children are like ships passing in the night. Again, financial wealth can exacerbate the situation. When a teenager has his or her own wing of the house, entertainment, vehicles, and so on, then the need to interact with parents becomes almost nil. The response is to be intentional in making time together, from an early stage of your children's lives, and then sticking to some of those habits even when they are resistant teenagers. Perhaps it is dinner each night. Perhaps it is a weekend ritual. Maybe it is the drive to school. This is also an area where financial capital can be extremely helpful, as in spending on desirable vacations together. Whatever form it takes, make the time to spend the time together and learning will follow—their learning from you and your learning from them.

Managing Privacy

Most parents procrastinate communicating with their children about family financial capital. The motivation is simple: None of us wants to harm our children, and most parents fear that if a child learns about family money, that discovery will demotivate or otherwise knock the child off course.

While understandable, this stance carries with it significant opportunity costs. It precludes making the most of the teachable moments we have described above. It also implicitly teaches children that money is taboo. This taboo can make it very hard for adult children to integrate wealth successfully into their lives.

The steps that we have outlined provide a foundation for that integration. Also, taking these steps begins to teach children ways to manage information about their family's private matters. As they grow, people around them (friends, younger family members, even teachers) may ask them or make comments to them about their family's wealth. If they have been prepared by speaking with you, they will feel more comfortable responding to others appropriately and without shame.

CHAPTER 15

Prenuptial Agreements

Introduction

Around 40 percent of first marriages in the United States, 60 percent of second marriages, and 70 percent of third marriages end in divorce.[1] Despite those numbers, only about 10 percent of married people believe that they have a chance of getting divorced, and over 60 percent of people believe that just bringing up the possibility of a prenuptial agreement would increase their chance of divorce. It is not surprising, then, for engaged couples who are presented with the idea of getting a prenup to say, "This feels like negotiating the end of my marriage before it's even begun!"

Nonetheless, it is important for couples at least to consider a prenup, especially when financial capital or a family business is a factor. In what follows we'll review the basics of what a prenup is and the process for talking about it as a couple. We'll add some considerations for parents who want to raise the topic with their adult children but are concerned about doing so. Our goal is not to argue for or against prenups but to help couples and families think and talk productively about this important topic.

Sadly, for too many families, the prenup discussion takes a toll on members at a time when they should be feeling great joy. We hope to orient this legal and financial process toward its proper end: the growth of the new family's qualitative capital.

---

[1] Based on United States Census data, as interpreted through the Centers for Disease Control National Vital Statistics System: http://www.cdc.gov/nchs/nvss/marriage divorce_tables.htm.

What Is a Prenuptial Agreement?

Marriage is a freely chosen state. But it takes place under state law, which brings with it obligations that you would not necessarily choose, especially around the treatment of property. For example, some states define all property acquired during marriage as "community property," held jointly and divided equally in case of divorce. Most states give judges discretion to divide marital assets "equitably," which usually involves considering the length of the marriage, the contribution to acquiring the assets, and each spouse's financial condition. In the case of the death of a spouse, some states require that the surviving spouse receive one-third of a deceased spouse's estate, known as an "elective share."

A prenup is a contract between prospective spouses to modify the terms of their marriage that would otherwise be governed by state law.[2] By using a thoughtfully drafted prenup, prospective spouses enter marriage knowing what will happen to property in the case of divorce or death.

Common reasons for creating a prenup include:

- Defining separate property (which belongs to one or the other spouse prior to and after the marriage) versus marital property (which is shared by the spouses).
- Protecting each spouse's separate property from division in the case of divorce.
- Protecting assets—such as business interests, real estate, or heirlooms—that one spouse considers part of his or her family legacy.
- Setting forth what each spouse can expect in terms of inheritance or insurance benefits in the case of the death of the other spouse.
- Protecting each spouse from debts that the other spouse incurred before the marriage.
- Protecting the interests of children from a prior marriage.
- Avoiding potentially large legal fees, publicity, and years of emotional turmoil that could come with a contested divorce.

Fundamentally, a prenup is about choices: giving the partners a choice about what happens to their property in the case of death or divorce rather than leaving those choices to a judge or relying on the default position under

---

[2] See http://brandongaille.com/18-interesting-prenuptial-agreement-statistics/, August 14, 2014; retrieved September 9, 2016.

state law. In the case of divorce, a prenup does not make it easier to end the marriage, but it can make it less painful by eliminating the need for some decisions, allowing both partners to move on with their lives sooner.

To be enforceable as a contract, a prenup comes with some basic requirements:[3]

- Even though drafted by attorneys, it must be written and signed by both parties with proper witnesses (such as a notary).
- Both parties must have the capacity to enter a contract.
- They must do so voluntarily, not under any sort of compulsion.
- Before signing the agreement, the parties must have provided each other full disclosure of their assets and their liabilities. Assets may include savings, real estate, stocks and bonds, retirement funds, as well as vested trust interests and expected inheritances. This step could require parents and grandparents to disclose to the couple the trust interests that they have vested in their child or grandchild.
- While theoretically a prenup could include agreements about pretty much anything (such as who does the dishes), courts will not enforce prenups that include terms that are illegal or repugnant to public policy (such as forbidding pregnancy, waiving child support, or requiring that children be raised in a specific religion) or that are grossly unfair to one party.

Some of these points are common sense, but in the emotional and logistical flurry leading up to a wedding they can be overlooked. For example, many states may consider prenups that are signed shotgun-style just before a wedding as executed under compulsion. As a result, a prenup ideally should be finalized several months before the ceremony.

The requirement for disclosure is perhaps the largest hurdle for most couples and their families. Intentionally hiding significant assets or liabilities during the prenup process will make the prenup unenforceable. Everything must be disclosed. That means that parents or grandparents who have not yet even informed their child or grandchild could find themselves being forced to make such disclosures—to both the child and the child's prospective spouse.

When it comes to the actual document, many prenups may look the same at first glance; nevertheless, it is important to read the terms carefully

---

[3] These, and all the other considerations raised in this chapter, are highly fact-specific. Readers should seek their own competent counsel in considering their personal or family situation.

and make sure that they accord with your wishes and circumstances. In general, the document will include:

- The date of the agreement and the names (and often the social security numbers) of the parties to it.
- Recitals: a list of "whereas," which states that the parties willingly and knowingly enter into the agreement and that it will supersede the rights that they may have otherwise had under state law.
- Articles: these are the heart of the agreement.

  o The articles will usually include a definition of separate property, which is the property that belongs to each spouse separately, before and after the marriage.
  o The articles will define the termination events that will trigger the agreement. An example of a termination event might be a spouse's filing for divorce.
  o Finally, the articles will specify what happens after a termination event, such as the sale of the marital home, the separation of separate property, and the division of marital property.

How Best to Approach a Prenuptial Agreement

The most important ingredient for a successful prenup is time. Time is required to make sure that the prenup is deemed enforceable rather than forced. More important, time gives the partners a chance to think through what the prenup means to them and their marriage.

For prospective spouses, we recommend considering and discussing the following two questions:

1. Are there specific terms in a prenup that would be especially important to me?
2. What do I most want to share with my prospective spouse about this process? What do I most want to learn from my prospective spouse?[4]

---

[4] The authors are grateful to Charles Collier, former senior philanthropic adviser at Harvard University, for many of these questions and those that follow. For more, see Collier's "Prenuptial Arrangements as a Family Conversation," http://docs.wixstatic.com/ugd/fab6ba_1de2cfc c0fe4cf5f40e2515f7e88e976.pdf.

Prospective spouses may find it helpful to think and talk about these questions even before they meet with their attorneys and begin drafting the prenup. Pursued this way, the prenup process can feel like something that the prospective spouses *own*, rather than an unwelcome imposition.

Prospective spouses may also find it helpful to speak with a counselor as part of this preliminary process. Marriage is already a life-changing commitment. Add in significant financial capital, and the emotions and questions it raises can feel overwhelming. Counseling over a series of months prior to the marriage could be a true investment of the family's financial capital in its human capital.

For Parents of the Prospective Spouses

So far, we have approached the prenup process from the standpoint of the prospective spouses. The reality is that few couples, especially in first marriages, raise the topic of prenups on their own. In most cases, parents ask their son or daughter to get a prenup. This is often the case when the family of one spouse has more financial wealth than the family of the other.

There are ways for parents to deal with this delicate situation. First, parents should acknowledge that, in most cases, their desire for a prenup has little or nothing to do with the couple and much more to do with their family's financial capital. Acknowledging this point can depersonalize the prenup.

Next, parents should be honest with themselves about how much or how little they have already informed their adult child about the family wealth. This is usually a very difficult step for parents. Yet more and more state law requires parents (or grandparents) to disclose vested trust interests or expected inheritances. The disclosure process may be the adult child's first serious introduction to the specifics of the wealth. It is natural for parents to feel anxious about having this money conversation with their adult child, especially as they face the prospect of a new family member (the prospective spouse) entering the family system.

Parents should then get clear about the realities, both external and internal.

The external realities include the disposition of the family's financial resources. When it comes to those resources (leaving aside whatever the prospective spouses currently own or are likely to earn), it is important to ask, to what degree is a prenup even necessary?[5]

---

[5] Again, these, and all the other considerations raised in this chapter, are highly fact-specific. We reiterate that readers should seek their own competent counsel in considering their own personal or family situation.

More and more parents give to their children during their lifetimes, and more and more gifts are made in trust. If those trust interests and family business interests are taken out of the equation, the adult child may have few financial resources that would become the subject of a prenup.

Just as important is the internal reality that parents feel. This is where parents themselves can benefit from thinking about and then talking over such questions as:

- What makes me want—or not want—my child to have a prenup?
- What personal history or beliefs affect my thinking about prenups?
- Would I be willing to leave this decision to my son or daughter?

If, after this process, parents do decide that they both believe it is important to talk with their son or daughter about a prenup, then there are some strategies that can make this process less potentially damaging than it may at first seem:

- Ideally, have the initial prenup discussion long before any of your children become involved in a serious relationship. This way, it cannot be taken as a judgment about any particular boyfriend or girlfriend.
- It may help to emphasize family legacy and tradition. For example, "We use prenups because we want to make sure that our family enterprise remains a family legacy. We see ourselves as stewards of these assets, not just as owners, and they benefit not just us but other family members, present and future."
- As hard as it is, as a parent, don't try to manage the prenup process alone.
- Parents often recommend legal professionals to their children and the prospective spouses. Give those recommendations some thought. Try to recommend not just the attorneys you know best. Think about how the prospective counselors' ages, genders, geographical locations, and expertise may fit with your child and his or her partner.

Again, many parents and adult children feel that the prenup process is imposed on them—out of fear. Our hope is that some of the ideas and actions described in this chapter can help you—if you decide to pursue a prenup—to keep your eye on the goal of using it to grow your complete family wealth, not just protect your financial capital.

CHAPTER 16

Getting Started

Questions

When considering the journey of family wealth, one of the main questions that family leaders ask is, "Where do we begin?"

In this book, we suggest that the most important activity to begin with is reflection: reflection on your intentions, your family culture, and the development of your family enterprise. Reflection on the big questions is the basis for any thoughtful action.

To aid in that reflection, we often begin by inviting our family members to ask themselves questions. There is no single list of the best questions to ask; which questions are most relevant and helpful will depend on where you are in your life, where your family is in its journey, and what role you play within that journey.

However, having discussed such questions many times with many clients over many years, we know that some rise to the top in terms of prompting fruitful reflection and discussion. We share here some of the questions that you may want to consider beginning with. Reflecting on these questions by yourself is a great preparation for then discussing them with additional family members. For a more comprehensive list of such questions along with chapters written by leading thinkers addressing each question, please see our *Wealth of Wisdom: The Top Questions that Wealthy Families Ask* (Wiley, 2019).

Questions for Reflection

- Do I consider myself wealthy? What does wealth mean to me?
- What do I see as the main factors in living well?
- What would I like my legacy to look like?
- How much financial wealth would I like to leave my children, and when?
- What beliefs do I hold about inherited money?
- How best can our family make decisions together?
- What are the challenges that my family faces in communicating with each other, and how might we overcome those challenges?
- What makes my family unique or different?
- Who do I trust most to advise me in making decisions about my business, financial wealth, or family?
- What of my family heritage would I like to see us hold onto? What should we let go of? What new practices or ideas might we take on that will serve us well in the future?

Practices

Beyond reflecting on and discussing these questions, there are many action steps that a family can pursue to begin the work of growing its complete family wealth. We have detailed such actions in the pages that have preceded, and several more (such as holding family meetings) are to come in the pages that follow.

At this point, we want to highlight three practices that we believe are most helpful to families that are starting on the journey of complete family wealth. We hope that you can incorporate them into your journey as soon as possible:

1. *The Three-Circle Model of Family Enterprise*: we describe this conceptual tool and its uses more fully in Chapter 2. It envisions every family enterprise as a combination of Family, Owners, and Managers. We recommend using it to orient yourself and your family members to the different relationships that make up your family enterprise. It is a great tool to use to identify where you are spending your time and energy, where you are not, and where you would like to. It can also help you categorize different sorts of decisions and to begin to disentangle nagging conflicts.

2. *The Three-Step Process of Family Communication*: we describe this process in Chapter 7. It is a simple but powerful way to make sure that communication is not impeded by "mind-reading" what we think other people are going to say to us. Very briefly, in this process, Step One is clarifying for yourself, in your own head, what you want to say; Step Two is for each person to share his or her thoughts, while others listen without interruption; and Step Three is to look for areas of common ground in the different views expressed upon which you can take action. You can use this process between spouses or partners, or among siblings, or with parents and children, and so forth.

3. *The Intergenerational Dialogue*: we talk about this practice more in the next chapter (Chapter 17, Family Meetings), but it is a practice that you can use outside family meetings as well—such as over dinner or during some "down time" on vacation. In this "dialogue," members of each generation that are present reflect, as a generation, on what they would like to learn from or ask the members of the other generation who are present, and what they would like to tell to or share with the other generation. Parents and children could do this exercise together, or grandparents, adult children, and grandchildren. After a few moments for reflection, each generation shares its questions and its statements with the other generation. The dialogue is meant to begin a conversation—there is no need to attempt to answer all the questions that are raised. Those can be recorded and saved for future family discussions.

CHAPTER 17

Family Meetings

Preparation

Families meet about all sorts of matters related to financial capital. For example, many hold quarterly or annual meetings with advisers to go over investment performance. The agendas for such meetings are usually driven by the advisers, who also manage the meeting process.

Some families also have meetings to attend to their complete family wealth. Such meetings touch upon intangible matters, such as values, wishes, concerns, even conflicts. As such, they can be wonderful and they can be challenging. The family must own the agenda. And managing the process usually requires a fair degree of preparation and skill. As a result, most families approach holding a true family meeting or a family retreat with some anxiety.

This chapter aims to reduce some of that anxiety and to give you a clear road map for considering whether and how to have a true family meeting. For the purposes of this chapter, we will use the single term "family meeting" to cover everything from a half-day gathering to multiday family retreats. What matters here is not so much the length of the meeting but its purpose: it is a meeting for and by the family, not driven by someone else's agenda. It is about complete family wealth, not just financial capital.

The key to a successful family meeting is preparation. Every family meeting should be preceded by several weeks—if not months—of lead time. Families can use this time to:

- Identify family members' shared goals and the topics that they want to take up at the family meeting.
- Craft and disseminate a clear agenda that flows from the Executive Summary.
- Prepare materials needed to support the agenda, such as financial statements, investment reports, foundation grant reports, and recommended readings.

Families are often surprised at how much time and effort must precede a family meeting. The more effort a family invests before a meeting, deciding and clarifying what to cover, the more productive the meeting will be. Also, all participants will enter the meeting with clarity about what will be covered and what is expected of them.

Through helping families design dozens if not hundreds of family meetings, we have found that taking the time beforehand to answer some questions can make all the difference. We divide these questions, and this chapter, into the Why, What, Who, When, How, and Where of family meetings.

Why?

Most families don't have family meetings. So why do it?

The answer is that family meetings are one of the most important tools a family of wealth can use to grow its complete wealth. It is not an exaggeration to say that every family that succeeds over multiple generations makes some use of family meetings.

Well-run family meetings can be used for at least three purposes:

1. Remaining connected.
2. Helping family members learn.
3. Making important decisions together.

Regular family meetings provide a forum for sharing news, concerns, opportunities, and challenges in an open and direct way. Family leaders can deliberate about and make shared decisions in a truly collaborative manner. Meetings offer the chance to help younger family members learn the basics of family finances and family traditions.

What to Do in a Family Meeting?

A clear agenda and defined goals are crucial. Without a clear agenda, meetings can meander and bog down, so that members may become frustrated or leave feeling that important business was left undone.

The activities at a family meeting are as varied as the reasons for having a family meeting. However, some of the more common things that we have seen families do at family meetings include:

- Asking individual family members to update each other on what's going on in their lives, their personal goals, and their plans.
- Conducting values-clarification exercises. One exercise we have seen families enjoy involves each member reflecting on and answering the question, "What matters most to me and why?" Families we know have also used the question, "What does a life well spent look like?" To discuss this question, we have had older family members gather in a group and come up with their answers. The rising generation family members gather together separately and imagine what their answers would look like if they were, say, 50 years old and looking back on their lives up to that point. Then both groups come back together and share their thoughts. Another exercise we have used with families involves first defining, together, what they see as the family's "founding values." Then, each generation separates to define, from their perspective, the family's "present values." From the combination of founding and present values, the family can decide to make a Family Values Statement. This statement does not need to be set in stone; it can change as the family's present values change.
- Telling stories, such as how individual members made their start in business or philanthropy.
- Learning about each other's styles of communicating. Such exercises can be quite fun as well as eye-opening. It can be especially fun to ask spouses or other family members to guess each other's communication styles.
- Learning about each other's preferred ways of learning, desired work, personalities, and preferred ways of relating to trustees.
- Reviewing the family's business operations or the family's wealth structures and their current performance.
- Visiting recipients of the family's charity together.
- Learning about each other's roles within the family enterprise. One particularly fun way of doing this learning is to have a collection of hats available, and then asking family members to put on a hat if they are a parent, a child,

a trust creator, a trust beneficiary, a director in the business, a manager or employee, and so forth. Some family members quickly find themselves with four or five hats perched on their heads!

- Learning about each other as members of different generations. As mentioned in Chapter 16, we call this the "intergenerational dialogue." Each generation in the family breaks into its own group and answers for itself these questions: "What would I like to share with the other generation?" and "What would I like to learn from the other generation?" The groups then reconvene and share their questions. Imagine hearing from your parents what they would like most to share with you or asking your children what you would like to learn more from them. It is a truly powerful exercise.

Who to Have at a Family Meeting?

Simply put, the list of participants should follow from the goals of the meeting.

If a primary goal is resolving conflicts or building a team, it may be important to limit the attendance to family members and a few facilitators. If, on the other hand, the meeting will cover various technical issues, experts may be present for some portions of the event. Examples include lawyers, accountants, investment advisers, and even family business or human resources consultants.

If the goal is to encourage connections across the generations, engage in family philanthropy, or to develop future leadership, then having adolescents and young adults present makes a great deal of sense. Elders may also be present to provide wisdom, continuity, and guidance as well as a voice for the family's heritage and legacy.

Children below the age of 14 can find it difficult to sit through a lengthy family meeting, so childcare arrangements are important. However, for larger family retreats, it can be a great idea to develop separate activities appropriate to children or teens, such as learning certain money skills, doing a group charitable project, or even just going on a hike together. Someday these cousins will be the adults running the family meetings themselves.

As we discussed in Chapter 7, many families grapple with the question of inviting spouses to a family meeting. Again, their inclusion should flow from the goals. If the goal is to share specific estate planning information, it may make sense for biological family members to meet first to decide together how to share information more broadly. If the goal concerns educating the rising generation, then naturally spouses should be present as key players in that work.

Another question that often arises is whether to have an outside facilitator. When just getting started and for more complex cases, a facilitator can make sense. When a family is facing a crisis, a facilitator may be invaluable. Many families also use a facilitator or consultant for their first few meetings and then gradually take over the reins. Families with whom we have worked for years may run their own quarterly or semiannual conference calls and ask us to facilitate an annual or biannual family meeting to help them "tune up" their relationships or learn new skills.

When to Hold a Family Meeting?

Time is another central element of family meetings. A meeting may take place for an afternoon, a day, a weekend, or several days. The length depends on the agenda, its complexity, and the size and dynamics of the family.

Often, families try to jam too much into one day, at the end of which members feel exhausted. If you have a lot to cover, we recommend splitting the material into two half-day agendas. You can meet from, say, 10 a.m. to 1 p.m. each day, with an afternoon and evening break between the two working sessions. This break gives individuals a chance to recharge and connect with each other informally. The break may also lead to insights or questions about the first day's material that then can be addressed in the second day's session.

Family meetings can help families in any stage of development. They are especially crucial during difficult transitions, which may include the sale of a business, a leadership succession, or the death or disability of key family members. Families who meet as a regular practice have a leg up in facing such challenges.

Regular family meetings also give families a chance to celebrate positive transitions. An annual meeting can include time to welcome new members of the family or to congratulate new parents. It can be an occasion to celebrate coming-of-age or promotions to leadership positions within the family enterprise. Making time for these celebrations shows everyone that this family pays attention to its key resource: its people.

The family's current needs and state of development determine the frequency of meetings—quarterly, semiannually, or annually. Generally, when a family is just starting the process of meetings, it can make sense to meet every six months for a few times. Once things are up and running, an annual meeting may be enough. Frequency may also depend upon how often the family connects in between the meetings on a formal or informal basis.

Finally, timing within the meeting is crucial. Again, people overestimate how much they can absorb in one sitting. Good practice is for the family to take rest breaks frequently, ranging from mid-session coffee breaks to longer opportunities to walk, nap, or exercise.

How to Run an Effective Family Meeting?

Have you ever been at meetings where attendees were only half there or everyone talked over everyone else? A family meeting requires focus and attention to achieve its goals. Families need to take steps to make sure their most crucial assets—family members—are ready and able to meet effectively.

First, planning for childcare is often a crucial step in making all participants feel comfortable.

Second, it is important to keep in mind that different people learn in different ways:

- Some find it easiest to pore over large amounts of text or numbers before the meeting.
- Others may be visual learners and benefit from flip charts or illustrated slides instead of text.
- Most people digest many smaller portions of information better than trying to take in large amounts of data in an extended sitting.

Too many families also forget that a meeting should be just as much about listening as about talking. For example, many parents use family meetings to disclose information about their estate plans or holdings to their adult children. But that information comes with emotional weight. Make sure you always give people at a meeting a chance to process what they hear, and to react and respond.

Of all the elements needed for a successful family meeting, solid ground rules may be the most important. (See the sidebar on ground rules at the end of the chapter.) You may want to use some of your first family meeting to discuss and decide upon the ground rules for meeting together. It may seem strange to impose rules on a family event. Yet, as with any social etiquette or code of conduct, a healthy set of rules exists not to stifle love and care but to help us express them.

One thing every family should remember about ground rules is that, once adopted, they must be upheld. In the heat of a discussion, members will inevitably start to break the rules. What's crucial is how the family responds. Having to stick to the rules just like everyone else offsets any sense of entitlement. The rules are living testimony that, although wealthy, the family acts responsibly and respectfully to all people.

Sometimes even with good ground rules, conflict arises in family meetings. In this case, it helps to have an outside facilitator to manage the conflict. Whether you have a facilitator with you or not, there are steps for dealing with conflict in a productive manner:

- Distinguish between healthy disagreements and inappropriate levels of conflict. Ask yourself, "Is this disagreement generating good discussion or getting in the way of the meeting's effectiveness?"
- Seek first to understand and then to be understood. Ask questions that aim to clarify what others are saying before responding.
- Name the source of the conflict as you see it and ask the group to do the same. For example, conflict may come from miscommunication, different needs or interests, differences in values or beliefs, or an ineffective structure. If you put a name on the source of the conflict, and others affirm that is the problem, then the group is well on the way to resolving the conflict.
- Refer to the ground rules that are relevant to avoiding or resolving conflict. Examples might include: listen, be respectful, or own your own views.
- Look for common ground. Maybe you disagree about how much to give to a certain organization, for example, but you can affirm your shared interest in philanthropy or to a certain charitable sector. Affirming common ground will take some of the sting out of the conflict.
- Remind others (and yourself!) that it is okay to have different values and opinions.
- Take a break. When it seems that the group is getting nowhere, take a short breather for everyone to restore calm.

For some additional tips on how to navigate conversations about strongly held differences of opinion, see the section at the end of this chapter.

Where to Hold the Meeting?

Family meetings are special events. Many families look back upon specific meetings as turning points in their development and attach special meaning to where these occurred. Often family retreats become part of the family's collective memory and traditions. They should occur in special places.

Parental homes or offices often come with baggage. Meeting at home may encourage family members to fall back into old patterns of behavior, plus it may be intimidating to in-laws or to children less familiar with the location.

Gathering family members at a resort, a rented home, or a country club costs money that is well spent. Using the family's resources for a meeting sends an important message to the family. It says, "We are here not just to grow the money but to grow ourselves, to grow together."

The facilities should allow for recreation in addition to business. People work together most effectively when they feel good about themselves and each other.

Places for family retreats should be convenient to everyone who needs to attend. It is not fair to expect members to attend and then make attending a hassle. Other matters of convenience to keep in mind include:

- Making sure bathrooms are easily accessible and adequate in number.
- Reducing noises that may obstruct hearing, particularly for older family members.
- Using an audio system so all can hear and speak clearly.
- Giving attendees traveling from afar time to rest before the meeting.
- Arranging for adequate meals and drinks.

Wise families recognize that a family meeting is not just about the content to cover. It is about the process, the place of the meeting and the memories it creates. A well-chosen and prepared environment can add immeasurably to the family's comfort and productivity.

SAMPLE GROUND RULES

Be present
Demonstrate your respect and commitment by setting aside potential distractions. Turn off electronics. If you need to be reached in case of emergency for your children or business, designate a contact person. Be present at the scheduled start time so the meeting can get the job done. Devote room in your life and your heart to this meeting.

Be respectful in words and action

Speak respectfully, pay attention when someone else is talking, and avoid jumping in to finish sentences. Avoid negative body language such as eye-rolling, shaking heads, or other indications of emotional reaction unless you follow up by talking directly about your reaction. Keep profanity to a minimum. If you have a question or point to make, wait for an opening or raise a hand to indicate you have something to bring up. You will appreciate it when others do that while you are talking.

Listen

Listening is a skill that must be practiced, but it pays off tremendously. Be willing to demonstrate you understand what the other person is saying before making your own point. You may find you are reacting to what you *believe* someone said, not what was really said. When someone else is saying something that you disagree with, make sure you are listening to what is being said.

Be patient

Recognize and accept that, with limited time overall, not all comments or questions must be dealt with right away. Be willing to let some things go. Pick the issues you think are most important. Over time, it is likely that the important things will get dealt with.

Own your views

Make "I" statements rather than broad, global statements that imply you know the truth or that something "is obvious." Saying "everyone knows that is ridiculous" is unhelpful. Saying, "I really disagree with what you just said," is more honest and may be more accurate. If others do share your views, it will be clear there is a shared perspective on an issue. If it turns out your view is not shared by others, you may then open yourself to new viewpoints or solutions.

Be willing to edit what you say

Saying anything and everything you feel under the guise of honesty can simply be a license to attack. Deliver your points with tact and respect. Appropriate editing of your message will make you more likely to be heard. It will also reduce the chances that other people will get defensive.

Strategies for Communicating Effectively about Difficult Topics

1. General principles
   - Everyone shares responsibility for the success of the communication.
   - Trust each other's goodwill.
2. Helpful reminders
   - Raise hands to indicate that you wish to speak.
   - Be aware of tone: not what you say but how you say it matters most.
   - Be ready to forgive.
   - Play together! Sharing fun times makes it easier to talk about difficult topics.
   - Use a "Parking Lot" to keep track of ideas or actions for which we don't have time to discuss now, but that we don't want to forget.
3. If you're feeling stuck: Distinguish between "process" and "content."
   - As a rule of thumb, if you find you're having a hard time in a conversation, switch from the content to the process: what is going on inside me, or inside us, or between us, that may be causing the challenge?
4. Be aware of
   - Your feelings—are you starting to feel emotion (such as anger, hurt, sadness)?
   - Your behavior—are you withdrawing, getting confrontational, becoming more vocal, deflecting with humor?
   - The other person's or people's feelings and behavior—how are they responding (again, with withdrawal, confrontation, etc.)?
   - Decision-making procedures. If these are unclear, ask for clarification.
5. Practice these five key steps:
   - Listen respectfully, without interruption. Share back what you believe that you have heard for clarification and validation.
   - Ask clarifying questions. ("Could you say more about . . .?")
   - Share your own views as your own, with "I" statements.
   - Identify areas of agreement.
   - Agree on next steps and a plan to address areas of difference.

CHAPTER 18

Family Stories and Rituals

The Stuff of Life

Every family has stories. Much of life *is* stories, a collection of stories. If you want to learn about what's under the ground, you can, so to speak, start digging and look for yourself. But none of us remembers our birth or even our first few years of life. We certainly can't remember what took place before we were born. We depend on stories from our parents and others to fill in our sense of where we came from. In turn, these stories shape how we think about where we are and where we are going.

We have emphasized at several points in this book the special importance of stories for family with significant wealth. Financial capital can sometimes feel like it's the whole story. Or, conversely, it may lower a shroud of silence on the family. In either case, a family that hopes to preserve its complete wealth over time must learn to keep its stories alive. That is the only way the family itself will continue.

While everyone likes stories, sometimes families find it hard to get the ball rolling in telling family stories. Here are some questions that we have seen prompt storytelling at family meetings. If you are going to ask a specific family member to share some stories at an upcoming meeting, perhaps give him or her this list beforehand to prepare:

- Who is someone that played a significant role in your life? How did this person shape your life, perspectives, and values?

- What are some of the important lessons you have learned in your life?
- Reflecting on your past, which of your accomplishments do you find the most gratifying and are you most proud of?
- What has been your greatest challenge thus far? What did you learn from this experience?
- Which of your stories, values, and beliefs would you most like to maintain and pass on to future generations?

It can be incredibly powerful to discuss these questions and to come to recognize the impression that these stories make on ourselves and those around us.

It can also help to recognize some of the themes that run through the most powerful stories in our families' lives. For example, many families preserve stories of failures, crises, or disasters, when the entire family had to uproot itself and start again. These stories teach themes of resilience and perseverance. They often also contain within them important descriptions of others' kindness toward family members, reminding the family that it has survived in part through others' goodwill.

Some families may feel it is not safe to tell stories, especially about money, because those stories may bring with them descriptions of entitlement, abuse, or conflict. However, sharing the hard stories is just as important as sharing stories of triumph and happiness. By showing children and other members of the rising generation that you can manage the emotions that hard stories bring up, you model mature ways of managing these negative emotions—ones that they, too, will have to deal with themselves someday. Indeed, in telling stories it is important not to make the tale too packaged or perfect. What makes a story compelling is often its quirkiness and the elements of surprise.

When it comes to sharing stories, we have seen families do so in a variety of ways:

- After a day-long family retreat, the patriarch or matriarch may gather everyone around a fire to tell a story from his or her youth. (Hopefully, not one that adult parents have heard 20 times before!)
- As a variant to that exercise, the oldest member of the family may tell a story that he or she remembers hearing from the oldest member of the family when he or she was a child. Such stories can capture a sense of the family's existence into the past for well over 100 or 150 years. Then the

family can point out that the youngest members of the family may very well tell that same story to their grandchildren, 70 or 80 years from now.

- As part of the intergenerational dialogue exercise (described in Chapter 17, Family Meetings), members of each generation may think of stories that they would like to share with members of the other generation, to illustrate a point they would like the other generation to understand about themselves.
- We have seen families in which members of the rising generation have asked their parents or grandparents to tell them stories about how they got started in business or philanthropy. It can be particularly fun to have members of the rising generation interview a grandparent using some of the questions listed on the prior page.
- Some families encourage storytelling by setting up a grandparent– grandchild lunch at every family meeting. This is a time when parents leave the room to allow the elder and the rising generation to connect in the wonderful ways that only they can when they are alone.
- We have also seen several families where members of the rising generation have asked their parents to tell them the "dirty secrets" of what it was like for them to be young adults. These are stories that may be best shared in private settings rather than at a family meeting!

Rituals

Rituals are closely related to family stories. Storytelling is a ritual act. And stories give shape to and justify rituals.

We have already emphasized the role of elders in family rituals. Here we will recapitulate a few thoughts on the importance of rituals to family life.

Rituals are different from ceremonies. Ceremonies—such as weddings, baptisms, or funerals—usually are marked by traditional, set words and deeds. But these ceremonies truly mark the end of the ritual and the start of a new stage of life. They are not the rituals themselves.

Rituals have three main parts.[1] The first is a break with the everyday course of life. It usually involves some sense of realizing that one cannot go

---

[1] See Arnold Van Gennep, *The Rites of Passage*, trans. Monica B. Vizedem and Gabrielle L. Caffee (Chicago: University of Chicago Press, 1960).

back to the old way and consequently imparts a sense of mourning. The second stage involves the creation of a space apart from the rest of life in which new knowledge can be developed or new information is shared with the participants of the ritual. Third is the re-entry of the participants into everyday life and the integration of what they have learned in that parallel space. This third stage is the one usually marked by ceremonies, which publicly indicate the start of the new stage of life.

Rituals may sometimes look silly, but they always serve a serious end. Here are some conspicuous examples:

- birth of a new member
- coming of age
- the marrying in of a new member
- creation of a new elder
- the death of a member

In all these examples, the point of the ritual is not to constrain members or limit their freedom but rather to lay the foundation for their future growth. If human beings grew like trees, in a steady, linear fashion, perhaps we would not need rituals. But our growth is discontinuous: we often break with past stages of life and need to jump to new ones. By providing a process for moving ahead, rituals create the conditions for true human freedom.

We have seen families use many rituals in the context of family meetings. A simple ritual is beginning and ending the meeting with a few words of hope and gratitude. Family members may also ask participants to go around the table and update each other on what's new in their lives since the last meeting. Another ritual is asking any member who is new to the meeting—young adults or new spouses—to share a few words about themselves and their dreams. In some families, these words are accompanied by a slideshow of pictures capturing important moments in that member's life. The same kind of ritual can be applied to family members who have passed away since the last meeting.

As an aside, aunts and uncles in a family are often central to the ritual of coming of age. In the context of significant financial capital, we have met many families in which an aunt or uncle—at the request of parents—was the first to speak to rising generation members about the specifics of the family's wealth. Aunts and uncles combine distance and closeness that allow them to navigate this difficult transition with both care and perhaps also some sense of fun and excitement. For the same reasons, aunts and uncles often find them-selves serving as informal mentors to their nieces and nephews as they navigate the transition to higher education, career, and independent family life. These are all aspects of coming of age, which are sometimes not celebrated enough in our modern world. The more we can do justice to the importance of these transitions, the more we can honor the important role that aunts and uncles often play in helping make them successful.

CHAPTER 19

Family Mission Statements

Why a Family Mission Statement Matters

As we saw in Chapter 2, a sense of shared purpose is key to family flourishing. This chapter describes what a family mission statement is, how to create one, and how to use the family mission statement effectively with your family.

Our studies of families that have flourished over generations indicate that one of the factors behind their success is that family members identify their core values and use those values to articulate a shared dream. This is what a family mission statement is all about.

Sometimes people distinguish more action-oriented mission statements from broader, more aspirational vision statements. We are going to use the term mission statement to cover both possibilities. As we mentioned in Chapter 17, some families produce values statements. As will be seen shortly, we see family values as intimately tied to family mission statements.

The family mission statement, as we are describing it, describes both the *why* of a family's shared effort as well as the *where to*. As Alice learned from the Cheshire Cat, if you don't care where you're going, you'll be sure to get there. The family mission statement ensures that your family isn't just wandering somewhere. But a statement that is not grounded in a firm sense of the family's values and vision will amount only to words on paper.

What Is a Family Mission Statement?

A thoughtful family mission statement articulates a shared sense of purpose, provides a comfortable basis for ongoing dialogue, offers guidance to rising generation family members as to what the family is all about, and incorporates each family member's unique thoughts, talents, and contributions. It may be a couple of lines or a few paragraphs. Whatever its length, it ideally tries to answer these four questions:

1. Who are we?
2. What do we stand for?
3. What do we want to do?
4. How will we accomplish our goals?[1]

A family mission statement will reflect the individual character of the family, its history and values, as well as the main areas of its shared efforts, for example, business or philanthropy.

Here are three examples of brief introductions to family mission statements:

1. Our family mission is to preserve and promote responsible stewardship by nurturing our passions for self, family, and community.
2. We want our capital to allow our children and their children to be able to find their passion and pursue it with excellence.
3. Our family mission is to prepare and uphold the values of our ancestors while encouraging independent thoughts and ideals in future generations to enhance the core values of our family.

A somewhat fuller introduction looks like this:

- Our family has made a conscious decision to remain connected. We believe that remaining together enables us to actively and purposefully:
  - Support individual members in discovering and pursuing their callings.
  - Support individual members in developing their gifts for the benefit of society.

---

[1] Leslie Dashew et al., *The Keys to Family Business Success* (Aspen, CO: Aspen Family Business Group, 2011).

Here is the beginning of the mission statement of a seventh-generation family enterprise that has set its sights seven generations into the future. The family's mission is:

To be a fourteenth-generation family company—financially strong, intellectually progressive, and deeply committed to the well-being of our businesses, our employees, our communities, and each other.

How to Create a Family Mission Statement

To endure and make a positive impact on a family, the mission statement usually is created by the whole family, not just by one member. When the patriarch or matriarch writes a mission statement on his or her own, even if it is approved by the larger family, it may soon disappear into a file folder and be forgotten.

There are exceptions to this rule. For example, Henry Phipps, the steel entrepreneur, wrote a brief letter to his son in 1911 outlining his wishes regarding the values and practices that should inform the management of their family wealth, a letter that still guides their family office to this day.

Since creating a family mission statement is a group effort, it is important to structure the process. It is best done in the context of a family meeting or meetings devoted to this task. We recommend taking several steps, with ample time for reflection and discussion.

The first step is to set a positive frame by thinking and then talking, as a family, about these questions: What is a time when each of us felt a strong sense of community or emotional connection as a family? What was it about that time that created those feelings?

With this sense of connection established, you can then discuss, as a family, questions like these:

- What are our core values as a family?
- Why do we want to stay together as a family?
- What family traditions do we want to preserve?
- What impact do we as a family want to have on the world?
- How much do we want to be connected, and how much do we want to be independent?

Discussing these questions can help to clarify the family's values. Family values are built upon the shared values of individual family members. One way to clarify the family's values is to use a set of cards with values words on them and allow members of the family to identify their top five values. Members can then share their lists and see which values appear on all or most members' lists.

An even simpler way, mentioned in Chapter 17, is for each family member to reflect on and answer the question, "What matters most to me, and why?" As family members go around the circle and answer this question, their personal values will become evident. These individual values can then be combined for a list of shared family values.

Once the family has a shared list of values, you can turn this list into a family mission statement. The list of values, perhaps with some explanation of what each value means to the family, can also serve as an addendum to the mission statement itself.

Brevity is a virtue in family mission statements; it can be hard to recall the mission if it is too long. At the same time, the family may want to create an appendix to the mission statement that defines terms used in it. Terms that commonly benefit from such definitions include "education," "work," "self-fulfillment," and the like.

How to Use a Family Mission Statement

Just talking about values and answering the question, "What matters most to me and why?" strengthen communication and shared understanding. Once you also have a family mission statement, you can then use that statement in a variety of ways.

For example, consider what parts of the larger family system the mission statement should touch and how. If a family has an operating business, the family mission statement can be adapted to express the family's desires for the business's impact on the world. In addition, a best practice for families with operating businesses is to establish a family council that expresses the voice of the family vis-à-vis the business; the family mission statement is a natural guiding principle for this body. A family mission statement may also inform a family's philanthropic decisions, whether through a family foundation or a donor-advised fund. Some families create family constitutions that link together all their operating entities and family council in a system of governance; a family mission statement often heads that document and gives direction to the procedures that follow. (For more on family governance and these structures, see Chapter 20.)

A simple use of a family mission statement is to read it aloud at the beginning of each annual family retreat or gathering, to remind everyone around the table of what really matters to them as a family. As your family grows and changes, it is natural to revisit and revise your mission statement. This exercise is a powerful way to reaffirm shared bonds and to clarify what really matters to you all.

Summary Worksheet

Now that you have read about family mission statements, you can use the space below to put this learning into action.

1. Identify your family's core values.

   _____

   _____

   _____

   _____

2. Identify some reasons for why you want to stay together as a family.

   _____

   _____

   _____

   _____

3. What traditions as a family do you want to preserve?

   _____

   _____

   _____

   _____

4. What impact as a family do you want to have on the world?

_____

_____

_____

_____

5. What would a draft of your family mission statement look like?

_____

_____

_____

_____

6. Identify upcoming gatherings or situations in which family members could discuss or be reminded of the family mission statement.

_____

_____

_____

CHAPTER 20

Family Governance

Humility and Freedom

If a family is going to institute some sort of governance structure, it should do so with a deep sense of humility. The agreements will not work without a sense of respect and freedom. The whole exercise will feel like make-work if it does not recognize that it serves things beyond the family: the well-being of its individual members and their ability to contribute to the good of the larger society.

For many families, humility leads them to recognize that what they need is not a governance system but, rather, clarity about decision-making in specific areas. Perhaps it is how they decide where to hold Thanksgiving each year. Or where to go for family vacation. It may be that they need to revisit their agreement on how to make decisions in a family foundation or they need to revisit the terms governing discretionary distributions in their family trusts. These are all examples of decision-making that do not necessarily require a system to tie them together. Achieving clarity in these matters might be the work of the communication practices or family meetings that we have described in the prior chapters.

Put another way, most families work best in a "confederal" way, in which each branch or nuclear family retains authority over most matters, while a few decisions are relegated to family-wide bodies. Such a confederacy preserves freedom while still honoring connection. Unfortunately, many advisers, motivated by founders' desire for control, prescribe more federal systems, with a strong bias toward centrality. For most families, that bias cannot survive the family's evolution.

What would family-wide matters look like in a confederal system? The oversight of a major operating business or family foundation could fall into that category. Also, it can be desirable to make sure that the family has a voice in the direction of such entities. A large family may also find it efficient to pool resources for helping family members learn about its enterprise, either the business or the wealth structures.

Family governance is a compact. It must be entered into freely. If people are to give up some of their freedom—as governance requires—they must feel that they are also gaining freedom thereby. The importance of freedom also means that governance is not a one-and-done sort of activity. Agreements must be renewed with each generation, in the creation of a new, horizontal social compact.[1] Each generation must ask itself, "Why are we doing this together? Why should we give up some of our freedom?" The founder's answer or the previous generation's answer is not good enough. If a governance system is not positively attractive to current and future generations, it will end up draining the family's social and spiritual capital, destroying the family in the end.

Constitution, Council, and Assembly

Governance is not the same as certain forms—literally, forms such as a family constitution or a foundation handbook.

To guard against this misperception, we find helpful a three-part distinction our colleague Patricia Angus devised, to distinguish three Ps in family governance:[2]

- *Principles*: the family's vision, mission, and values—the answers to the questions posed in Chapter 19. Everything else flows from these fundamental ideas.

---

[1] For more on the concept of the horizontal social compact, see Jay Hughes, *Family: The Compact Among Generations* (New York: Bloomberg, 2007), 129–135.
[2] Patricia Angus, "The Family Governance Pyramid: From Principles to Practice," *The Journal of Wealth Management* (Summer 2005), 7–13.

- *Policies*: here is where we find a family constitution or trust documents. These forms outline the rules for how the family makes decisions about important matters such as trust distributions, organization of a family council, or interactions between the family and an operating business.
- *Practices*: these may include some of the practices described in these pages, such as family meetings or the family executive summary process, or practices related to educating rising generation family members about wealth.

Principles are usually quite enduring, policies may change with major changes in the family's life, and practices can come and go as the family needs them. The key is to recognize that while practices may be the easiest to devise, they won't last or function well without a framework of policies, which, in turn, will never gain traction unless they are rooted in firmly held and agreed-upon principles.

If we turn to policies, the fundamental document in a family governance system is the family constitution. We have seen constitutions that are one or two pages long; we have seen others that are 50-plus pages long. The length reflects what the family seeks to achieve through the constitution. Here we will describe some of the main pieces along with examples.

A family constitution often begins with a statement of purpose. For example:

> *We, the members of the Smith family, have created this constitution to help our family grow and flourish through the generations. We believe that a thoughtful family governance system is essential to our well-being, as a family, and as individual members of that family. We hope that this constitution will be a living document, upon which both current and future generations will constantly reflect and improve, while continuing to honor our shared values and culture.*

Next, the constitution may offer a definition of the family—for example, as all the descendants of a certain ancestor, along with their spouses and children—as well as an expression of the family's values. This is where working beforehand to clarify those values is a crucial step. (For more on this step, see Chapter 19.) The constitution may also list the ground rules by which the family expects members to treat each other, especially when meeting together. (For a list of sample ground rules, see Chapter 17.)

The constitution then often sets out the central parts of the family governance system. These are usually the family assembly and the family council.

A **family assembly** is the body politic, the collection of all family members, at least those over a certain age. In most families, the main role of the family assembly is to elect the family council. Secondarily, a family assembly may be empowered to remove and replace members of the family council, increase or decrease the total number of family council members, and amend the constitution. More broadly, the family assembly provides a forum for the discussion of important family matters. It is meant to capture the spirit of the family, especially when it comes to making strategic decisions, such as to sell a legacy company or to make a large, new investment.

If the family assembly captures the spirit, the **family council** expresses the voice of the family. It is the family's executive body, its board—though it is important to distinguish between the family council and a family business board, if there is one. The family council answers only to the family, not to shareholders.

The family council usually has specific responsibilities enumerated in the constitution. Some of these may include the following:

1. Plan an annual open meeting during the annual family meeting, including an agenda of items to review with the family assembly and items of importance to the family for open discussion.
2. Provide recommendations to the appropriate governing bodies for appointment of trustees, officers, or directors to, say, family foundation boards, family office boards, or family trusts.
3. Annually review and approve budgets for itself and its committees.
4. Annually review and acknowledge receipt of the budgets of each of the bodies in the family enterprise, such as family foundations and family offices.
5. Review annual operating plans for all the parts of the family enterprise, and provide recommendations to their governing bodies based on this review.
6. Annually review the performance of the family governance system, implement such changes as it deems appropriate, and report to the family assembly.
7. Based on the foregoing reviews, recommend to the family assembly such amendments, if any, to the constitution or other governing documents as it determines to be necessary.

A family council usually has a chair and a vice-chair. It may also have subordinate committees, especially if it is charged with planning a regular family meeting. The family council may meet quarterly or monthly, depending on the extent of its duties. Family council members generally serve for at least three-year terms and are elected by the family assembly based on their life experience and their demonstrated commitment to the family, as shown through prior service.

As mentioned in Chapter 8, some families also institute a **wisdom council** as part of their family governance system. This body serves to convene family gatherings, tell family stories, and, when called upon, help mediate family disputes.

Design

Designing a family governance system takes time. As we will discuss shortly, the precursor is often something like the family executive summary process, which allows family members to share their views on the needs for and possible uses of a family governance system. Without doing something like this, it is hard or impossible to get family engagement in the plan.

Usually, much of the focus of family governance design centers around the family council, as it often sits at the center of the system, a mixture of deliberative, legislative, and executive body. Family councils come in all shapes and sizes, with varied responsibilities, as noted previously. To help you flesh out what your family council might do and how it might do it, here are some thoughts.

- What would be its primary purpose?
  - Organizing family meetings/events?
  - Collective decision-making?
  - Creating a sense of inclusiveness and a forum for input?
- What authority would it have?
  - Advisory only?
  - Authority to make decisions that potentially bind the broader family?
- How would the council be formed and structured?
  - How would the council members be selected or elected?
  - What criteria would define eligibility to serve?
  - How many members would it have?
  - How long would members serve?
  - Would there be officers?
  - Subcommittees?

- How would the council do its work?
  - How would meetings be conducted?
  - Would there be any formal procedures and protocols developed to govern council meetings?
  - How often would the council meet?
  - How would agendas be developed?
- How will the family council communicate and interact with the broader family?
  - Phone? Email? Text?
  - Family website?
  - Newsletter?
  - Agenda/minutes?
  - Report at family meeting?

Ratification

Again, designing and instituting a family governance system take time—and often the longer the better.

Usually, the family governance process starts with a family retreat, at which members may discuss such fundamental questions as, "Why do we want to stay together?" "What are the strengths and what are the weaknesses of our family culture?" "How do we want to treat each other?" "What would be the responsibilities of a family council, if we had one?"

If the decision is to pursue a governance system, then often a working group forms to begin to poll and engage the broader family. It may also be important for this working group to come up with a communication plan to share the basics of the plan with the broader family. As the working group begins to draft the constitution, it will be important to keep the family updated regularly and to test ideas with members outside the group.

Ratification of the new system comes at a family meeting specifically for that purpose. This meeting should focus on helping all members learn about the proposed plan and encourage a vigorous discussion. This is the point where, written constitution or not, the family truly begins to function as a family assembly. The vote on the constitution should be open and transparent, so that no one feels that they did not have a voice in the process.

Once the vote is taken and the constitution is approved, the family should also be prepared to celebrate its work. This is a crucial part of the process. The approval of a new constitution is a ritual step, and as such it should be treated as something out of the ordinary, something special. Here are some ways that we have seen families make their constitution ratification a special event:

- Start the event with a brief story from the family history.
- Start with reflective silence or prayer.
- Start with reading a meaningful poem.
- Have all family members sign a version of the constitution printed on vellum.
- Video the signing.
- Hang the signed vellum in the home of the youngest member of the family council (that way it will move over the life of the family, always residing with the rising generation).
- Plant a tree at the time of the signing, representative of the family and its growth together.
- Keep a family photo of the signers with the signed constitution.

Once the event is done, make sure to have the signed copy of the constitution nicely framed, and bring it to future family meetings. A reading from its preamble by a member of the family's rising generation may make a fine beginning to each family gathering.

The same event at which the constitution is ratified is likely also the time for the family assembly to elect its first family council. If so, then it is important for the constitutional working group to make sure that a slate of nominees is ready prior to the meeting. At the meeting, all members of the slate should have a chance to address the assembly, to share something about their experience in the family, and to explain why they would like to serve in this important role. Some families also ask family council nominees to submit a written statement explaining their interest before the election. Once the council is elected, it is important to take time to celebrate this important milestone in their lives and the life of the family.

Again, whatever form governance takes in your family, the key is to recognize the primacy of your family's culture. This culture will shape (or reject) whatever system you seek to apply. Over time, the system will also shape the culture. And that is the true benefit of family governance. When it works, it takes what may have been top-down, patriarchal structures and turns them into collaborative agreements; it refashions legal structures into relationships with human meaning; it transforms ambiguity into explicit and transparent agreements; it softens rigid rules or policies into principles and values that the family can interpret on a case-by-case basis; and it welds fragmented and disconnected documents into an integrated system.[3]

---

[3] For more on family governance, see Dennis Jaffe, *Governing the Family Enterprise* (Boston: Wise Counsel Research, 2017).

CHAPTER 21

Financial Capital

Return

This is not a book about investing in its own right. However, in the context of a family enterprise, oversight of the investment of financial capital is a prominent *family* activity, which also makes use of and has an effect on the family's qualitative capitals. As such, it behooves us to spend some time on investing as a human activity, and on some of the practices that we have seen families use effectively in their investing.

Investing has been going on as a popular pursuit since the eighteenth century, when certain government bonds became stable and marketable enough that they could be treated as "securities." It was key to the growth of the middle class, first in Europe, then in the United States, and today in many other parts of the globe. The availability of global markets for buying and selling shares in companies has been crucial to the creation of many—if not most—families' wealth.

There is a popular critique of investing today that it is a "loser's game." This line of thought argues that investing, as a mass phenomenon, undermines itself. People's attempts to beat the market make the market. Such attempts are not only self-deluding but they also expose the individual investor to loss. Empirical studies bear out this prophecy: individual retail investors who seek to time the market usually do worse than the market.

This critique of investing has been around for several decades. One response to it is the popular rise of indexing. Such investing seeks to dispel the delusion and openly describes itself as not *beating* but *being* the market.

Of course, indexing still exposes the investor to significant loss, as those indexers who bailed in the 2008–2009 or early 2020 downturns demonstrate. The individual human being, with passions, especially fear, can find it very difficult, if not impossible, to "be" the market.

The critics who described investing as a loser's game envisioned a different approach than indexing: one in which the investor steps away from focusing on financial return alone and sees himself as a human being—or representative of human beings—with human ends or purposes. To such a person, measurement by money or by money-averages makes no sense. Preserving financial capital—avoiding catastrophic loss—is one important goal. But there are innumerable other possible goals. Even the money-centered goal of "making a little bit of money every month" takes one out of the race of measuring oneself by a market average. It means being a person, not just with a point of view but also with your own purpose.

This critique of investing and this response—the response of seeking to "win the loser's game" by separating your personal goals and point of view from the mass market and its measures—explain why the rise of index funds and the rise of hedge funds have occurred simultaneously. These strategies initially look contradictory: Index funds seek to be the market, while hedge funds seek to differentiate themselves from the market. But it makes sense as two responses to the same critique. In fact, the hedge fund represents the more consistent response, as it seeks to "take a stand" or "express a point of view" or achieve specific ends apart from or even athwart the market.

It is no surprise that families with significant financial capital, who can afford to diversify across various platforms, tend to eschew broad-based, retail mutual funds and instead combine indexing for "core" positions with a variety of hedge or private equity funds to grow their assets.

Even so, both these approaches to investing—indexing and hedging—represent only partial responses to the basic critique. For that critique requires that investors cease to see themselves solely as investors, that is, as measurers of means. It requires owners to take responsibility for their ownership and define their own ends. Consider, for example, the significant attention to investment policy statements among institutional investors. An investment policy statement requires setting forth goals, risk tolerance, allowable types of securities, and so forth. Where does an investment policy statement come from? It is a product of a person, or a couple, or a family, or a committee. It is not a product of investing. That is, it is not a product of the science or art of investment management.

In other words, the contemporary critique of investing demands a reconsideration of oneself, one's ends or purposes, and one's relation to one's means and to others. Naturally, this step is one that far fewer investors have found it possible to take. Even those with investment policy statements on paper tend to find themselves asking each quarter, "What was my return? Did I beat the benchmark?"

In contrast, families that can take this step—who can focus on the ends and not just the means—have gone a long way toward making sure that their financial capital truly serves their qualitative capital.

Two Practices

For those families who can take this human approach to their investing, there are two enduring practices that we have seen make a huge impact on their return, understood in the broadest sense.

Investor Allocation

The first we call "investor allocation." Investor allocation is the allocation to each family member on the family balance sheet of that portion of the family's financial assets most likely to assist the long-term growth of those financial assets while minimizing estate, gift, or generation-skipping transfer taxation.

Most of us are familiar with modern portfolio theory and its admonition that 90 percent of successful long-term investing lies in correct asset allocation. Families who are successful investors have elaborate asset allocation plans. All too often, however, the individual family members holding these investments were not chosen based on how far they are removed from estate or gift taxation but rather by "who had cash" when the investment opportunity arose. Unfortunately for long-term tax avoidance, it is often the oldest member of a family who is wealthiest or "has the cash" when the investment opportunity arises. The result over time is that the oldest family members often hold many of the fastest-growing assets on the family financial balance sheet. And yet, the older members of a family are often the most risk-averse and would prefer to hold assets producing more income.

An investment program in which the oldest member of the family acquires growth securities brings a huge smile to the face of the Internal Revenue Service.

The IRS knows that if it waits patiently, it will collect more than half of the stock's growth as estate tax. The IRS, believe it or not, is sitting in the largest chair at the family table.

Investor allocation can reduce the size of the IRS's chair year after year, until it is the smallest at the family table, by reinvesting each new dollar of family wealth in the following way. Each time the family's investment adviser suggests a new investment, the family member, family office professional, or other adviser charged with investor allocation determines the investment's projected long-term growth rate. The "investor allocator" then chooses the family member or members who will make the investment based on estate tax implications. *Normally, this means the oldest family member buys the investments offering the lowest growth, and the youngest family member buys the investments offering the highest growth.*

Two investment classes can act as examples. Suppose the family wants to invest $100 in bonds that will be held to maturity and on which the family will receive current interest payments. This investment offers no growth of principal—the investor expects to receive, upon maturity, the same amount originally invested. Now let us suppose the family wants to invest $100 in venture capital. Let's assume the goal is to double the value of the investment over five years. The family will receive $200 for the $100 it invested, growing its principal by $100. Clearly the IRS would be delighted if Grandmother bought the venture capital investment, since the IRS will get upwards of $55 of that $100 profit upon her death. The IRS would be commensurately unhappy if Grandmother bought the bonds and a younger family member bought the venture capital investment. The IRS would be particularly unhappy if Grandmother bought the bonds and used them as collateral for borrowing by a grandchild who, without the loan, couldn't afford to make the venture capital investment. Grandmother is doubly happy since she will receive current income from the bonds, whereas she wouldn't ordinarily receive any return on the venture capital investment for five years. The family is delighted because Grandmother's estate didn't grow even though the family financial balance sheet grew by $100.

This example of investor allocation, while quite simple, makes the point. Obviously, there are many other types of investments, carrying varying degrees of risk, between the two categories we chose for the example. Every asset allocation program, properly made, will have investment classes throughout the risk universe. The point of investor allocation is to manage this risk universe by maximizing the growth of the overall family financial balance sheet while minimizing the growth of the individual portfolios most likely to be the next to be subject to estate tax.

To obtain maximum benefit from investor allocation, here are some issues a family will need to address.

- The family's mission statement should include a commitment to *long-term* growth in financial capital. Successful investor allocation requires that each family member elect to participate in investor allocation after careful consideration of his or her individual investment goals, as well as his or her commitment to the family's wealth growth strategy.
- Family members, directors of family philanthropies, managers of family investment vehicles, and trustees of family trusts should all agree to participate in the investor allocation program in the same positive spirit with which they participate in the family's overall asset allocation process.
- Families need bold trustees to implement an investor allocation program. Trustees have special legal responsibilities that govern their behavior as investors. Under these responsibilities, a trustee cannot give up ultimate discretion over the investment policy of the trust he or she oversees. The investor allocator will need to be mindful of those trustee responsibilities. Hopefully, the family trust instruments will grant the trustees the broadest possible investment discretion. Such a broad grant of investment authority will make it simpler for the trustees to accept their investment allocations within the family's overall asset allocation plan. The trustees' need for broad investment discretion is particularly necessary if higher-risk investments are to be allocated to the trusts.
- In constructing an investor allocation program, the youngest members of a family and the family's longest-term estate tax and generation-skipping-transfer-tax-free trusts should acquire the assets with the greatest growth potential. The portfolios of these family members and trusts should match the family's long-term or one-hundred-year investment horizon. The oldest family members should acquire the lowest-growth assets, to meet the family's 20-year horizon, and intermediate generations should take positions in accordance with the family's 50-year horizon. You will quickly comprehend that the plan works best when the youngest family members and the long-term family trusts that are exempt from estate taxation and generation-skipping transfer taxation have the most money, and the oldest members of the family the least. Obviously, this is not the normal situation; it is highly unusual. The problem, therefore, is how to get assets to the youngest family members and to the exempt long-term trusts so that they can make the desired long-term investments.

One way to solve the problem is with gifts. Unfortunately, gift tax law places low limits on how much can be given before taxes begin to accrue. The most successful strategy is for the oldest generation to make loans to the youngest generation—and in certain cases, after careful legal advice, to the tax-exempt long-term trusts—to enable acquisition of the appropriate assets. Intrafamily loans carry with them certain IRS responsibilities to ensure that they are arm's-length loans and not disguised gifts. A lending strategy should not be developed without proper legal and accounting advice to ensure that loans are not recharacterized as gifts. An important additional benefit of this strategy is the receipt of high cash flows by the oldest generation through their receipt of interest on their loans while the growth of a portion of their assets is capped. The additional cash flow will meet their desire for cash and provide them with additional liquidity to make gifts to family and philanthropy and to make additional loans. As with any investment decision, careful analysis of the role of such loans in the family's and the individual lenders' overall investment programs must be made to determine what portion of an individual's portfolio might be devoted to this program.

The Family Bank

The family bank is a practice that often goes together with the practice of investor allocation. It provides a means for a family's wealth to be leveraged by making loans available to family members on terms not available commercially. These are loans that would be considered high risk by commercial bankers but are low risk to the family because of their contribution to the family's long-term wealth preservation plan. Loans from a family bank are usually for two purposes: *investment*, to increase the family's financial capital; or *enhancement*, to increase the family's qualitative capitals.

In the case of loans for investment, the family's purpose is to take advantage of opportunities brought by individual family members. The loans afford the family opportunities to grow its financial wealth while enhancing the intellectual growth of individual members. These are frequently investments in businesses founded by individual family members. Such business loans follow these basic rules:

1. The borrower prepares a business plan and a loan application equivalent to that required by any commercial lender.
2. The borrower discusses the project's feasibility with the family bank's board and advisers.

3. When a loan is granted, the borrower provides proper business reports on the investment.
4. The borrower ultimately repays the loan.

This process gives the family borrower excellent business training and the highest possible chance of a successful financial outcome.

With enhancement loans, the family's purpose is to increase its qualitative capital by increasing the independence of individual family members. As with investment loans, proper lending procedures for enhancement loans are critical to the growth of each borrower's qualitative capital. When seeking an enhancement loan, the borrower should be encouraged to state how such a loan will increase his or her independence and how the loan will add to the family's human, legacy, family relationship, structural, and social capital. When family members explain to their peers and advisers on the family bank board how a loan will be enhancing, they must be certain that their individual qualitative capital will really be enhanced. With enhancement loans, repayment comes in the form of the increased independence of the individual borrower and his or her increased capital.

This may seem like a surprising point: that a *loan* could increase individual *independence*. The surprise is natural. Entered unwisely, a loan can create terrible dependence and resentment.

That is why families striving to preserve their complete family wealth quickly grasp that a family bank is not primarily about financial capital. While having a friendly lender gives an enormous competitive boost, it is the growth of qualitative capital that is the true reason for forming a family bank.

Because it is a delicate business, here are some guidelines for setting up a family bank.

- The family bank should not be a formal institution. It isn't a bank in the normal corporate sense. It is important that it be informal so that its activities remain private and so that it can evolve a system of governance that meets the unique circumstances of the family that creates it.
- The family bank must have formal rules for meetings. It should have officers, directors, and, if needed, advisory boards. It should have procedures for receiving and processing loan applications. That said, the rules and procedures will vary considerably, depending on who will fund the loans.
- The family bank must have a mission statement explaining its philosophy and reason for being. The lenders and borrowers must understand the family bank's purpose—to be a high-risk, low-interest lender—and the

consequences of that policy. The bank's mission statement should also contain a values section incorporating the overall family mission statement and should explain how the bank will assist in carrying out that mission.

- Because family trusts are potential lenders and borrowers, it is particularly important that trustees understand and agree to participate in the family bank.
- It is important to have concurrence of all family members, both lenders and borrowers, with the terms of the bank's mission statement.

It is particularly important that all family members who agree to participate in the family bank be given copies of all loan applications. Personal financial data may be withheld for confidentiality, but all members should receive the qualitative capital portions of the applications.

CHAPTER 22

Preserving a Family Vacation Home

Hard Questions

For generations, vacation homes have been a mark of wealth. These properties often become a substantial part of their owners' estates, financially and emotionally, leading to some hard questions: Do family members want to preserve the property as a true "family" vacation home? And if so, how?

The attraction to doing so is usually evident. The vacation home is likely in a beautiful location. The owners' children and grandchildren may cherish memories of spending time there each year. To use language from our book *The Cycle of the Gift*, a family vacation home is the most concrete and perhaps most powerful form of a "gift with spirit."

The challenges to preserving a family vacation home are also substantial. Real estate is illiquid and can be expensive to maintain. Jointly held property brings with it legal complexity. Most complex of all are the interpersonal issues of managing such property.

Competent counsel can help owners of the property foresee and address many complexities through appropriate structures for ownership and governance.

However, to adapt Peter Drucker's famous saying that, "Culture eats strategy for breakfast," we would say that culture eats structure for dinner. Not even the most creative documents will preserve a shared vacation home if the family does not attend to its human relationships—its "family culture."

What, then, does the family culture look like that increases the likelihood of successful, enjoyable preservation of a family vacation home? And how does a family inculcate and strengthen that culture?

Family Culture as the Solution

Culture is formed of habits and beliefs. Habits and beliefs arise, in turn, from modeling behaviors and communicating expectations. Most simply, if you want to achieve a certain result, then lead that life. If you want to preserve your vacation home, then you need to live a way of life that supports its preservation. That means practicing these habits yourself. It also means expecting others to practice them.

What does this life look like? Here we're going to borrow from the 100-Year Families Study, our research into families who have successfully passed on a major family enterprise through three generations of family ownership. These enterprises often involve operating businesses. Their practices apply directly to families who are managing other assets together, such as a vacation home. Some of the key elements of "100-Year" family culture include learning and sharing what you learn with your family members, developing the habit of regular and transparent discussion of financial matters within your family, trusting others and earning their trust, and modeling the expectation that all family members will, in their own ways, contribute actively to the family.

In addition, there are habits that we have seen prove instrumental for the specific task of preserving a family vacation home:

- Make sure that everyone shares in the duties of ownership, so that no one feels burdened as the sole "steward"—or entitled to an outsized voice in the property's management.
- Tell stories that connect the family members to the property. Why this place? What was here before us? What special events took place here? A great way to "tell" stories is by decorating the property with pictures of the past and present.
- Cultivate a sense that the property is special, something worth family members' devoting their time and money to. One way to do that is through holding a reunion there each year that also recognizes important milestones in family member's lives. Some families write their children's names or their own names on a certain wall of the estate, creating a record of the family for decades or even centuries. Others decorate the home with special

items purchased or made by family members. Some family vacation homes have guestbooks that stretch back decades, in which now-elderly family members can see records of their own visits as children.

- Another important habit of mind is to remind yourselves that the family and the property are not the same. Cultivating this habit will allow your family to deal with the time when someone asks to be bought out.
- Be a good host. Practice the habit of being enjoyable for others to spend time with, and help them be enjoyable to each other, so that they are grateful for the time together rather than feeling it to be a burden. This habit is especially important vis-à-vis significant others or spouses. If the spouses of younger family members enjoy visiting the property, they will bring their children, laying the foundation for a shared future.

Facing Realities

For most families, whether it is a good idea to try to preserve a family vacation home is an open question. There are benefits and costs. If such a culture does not or is not likely to take hold in your family, the best thing you can do may be to speak directly with your children about whether eventually to sell the property. We have seen many instances in which parents' willingness to raise this possibility has proven a great relief to the rising generation.

The most practical matter, then, may be first to step back from the question of *what* you're trying to preserve and *how* to preserve it, and to reflect honestly on the question of *who* you and your family are and whether this challenge is right for you.

CHAPTER 23

Family Philanthropy

The Benefits of Family Philanthropy

Philanthropy can powerfully assist a family in shaping its values and, through its organization and practice, it can also teach a family how to govern itself.

Philanthropy is, perhaps, the fundamental expression of personal and family values. If the family mission statement is an expression of these values, philanthropy is often the best way to move them into practice. Philanthropy can often be a means for family members who are isolated from society by their wealth to connect with the larger issues of the world and to find an active and meaningful place in it.

From Carnegie and the Astors, in the nineteenth century, to Gates, Buffett, and Zuckerberg today, American society has been blessed by the willingness of families to give back substantial parts of their wealth for the betterment of mankind. These individuals and families understand that philanthropy improves the lives of their family members and, most important, the lives of us all.

We are always impressed, when we speak to later-generation members of old families, by the pride expressed when they discuss their ancestors. These family members express great pride in the financial acumen of their forbears and appreciation for the financial benefits that have accrued to them as a result. There is, however, a special lilt to their voices when philanthropy is discussed. Many of the later-generation family members have continued the philanthropic work of their ancestors, albeit in fields of activity that their ancestors could not have imagined and, in some cases, would not have approved. The important thing is that family values of stewardship and giving back were inculcated in the family value system. Even more important, they are active values, calling for family members to participate in the world by sharing their qualitative capital and, where appropriate, their financial capital.

As Virginia Esposito, founder of the National Center for Family Philanthropy, has written, family philanthropy brings special gifts not just to families but to society at large. Here's what she says.

- Family philanthropists are in it for the long haul.

They are not focused on what produces impact this quarter or even just this year.

- At the same time, family philanthropy is often set up so that the family can act quickly and respond to immediate requests where needed.

Most families do not labor under the bureaucracies of large independent grant-makers.

- Families that engage in philanthropy can be a role model and/or guide for other families and individual donors.

Just consider the list of names shared at the start of this chapter.

- Families that engage in philanthropy help create and expand an overall culture of giving.

Philanthropy for the Family

In addition to its social benefits, family philanthropy creates benefits for the families who engage in it. To continue with Ms. Esposito's observations:

- Families that give together engage in multigenerational conversations.

Older generations pass along their legacy, lessons, and experiences to future generations. At the same time, the rising generation can share new ideas, new strategies, and new demographic realities.

- Family philanthropy is a medium for transferring values and family togetherness.

  Philanthropy provides the family with something to focus on that is positive and shared, rather than a question of "who gets what."

- Family philanthropy is an important tool to teach younger family members about the value of giving.

  Study after study suggests that giving begun early becomes a habit that lasts a lifetime.

- Family discussions about giving and values can create a sense of legacy or place.

  Entitlement means feeling that the world owes you. Legacy involves seeing yourself as part of a larger whole. Family philanthropy reinforces this feeling in a whole host of ways.

  While gifts of financial capital are important, it is the gift of human capital that is key to the use of philanthropy as a tool for long-term family wealth preservation. It is the sharing of self that makes philanthropy a critical contributor to the preservation of the human assets on the family balance sheet.

  Where does philanthropy fit in a family governance structure?

1. Every family mission statement should have a section dealing with the family's responsibility to the outside world and a section on how it will interact with the outside world.
2. Every family balance sheet should reflect the portion of the family's quantitative and qualitative assets devoted to philanthropy.
3. Every family with financial capital devoted to philanthropy should create a formal organization to support its giving. The form of organization should be determined in consultation with skilled advisers but, at a minimum, should include a broad structure that will allow participation in decision-making by all family members.

Getting Started

Many families also use the organization of a philanthropic entity as the first step in the shared journey of growing complete family wealth.

To start, if your family does not already come together to give, you may want to encourage each family member to reflect on these questions, and then meet to discuss your answers. The discussion can serve as the basis for starting to plan for shared giving.

- What was the tradition of giving in your family as you grew up?
- Does philanthropy feel like an obligation or a freely chosen act?
- Which charitable organizations do you support with your own time or money?
- Which organizations or charitable sectors are you are most committed to?
- Do you currently serve on the board of, or have other leadership roles in, any charitable organizations?
- Do you feel it is important to support charitable organizations at your death?
- Do you feel you are currently giving as much money to charitable organizations as you would like? If not, what would need to happen for you to give as much money to charitable organizations as you would like?

Philanthropy offers every family the chance to experience the joy of rediscovering its most important values and offers a family a way to share the thrill of helping others. It also tightens family bonds—the family glue—by recognizing and acknowledging the creativity and passions of each member.

As we have discussed throughout this book, the key to making family philanthropy work is to recognize the developmental stages of individual family members. Many parents try to engage their late-teen or early 20-something children in philanthropy. For some children, this works just fine. For others, the developmental need to make their own way in life outweighs the desire to "give back." Parents should understand this possible disconnect and not take it as a sign of a child's lack of care.

In addition, to engage young adults in philanthropy, make sure that the process feels open and inviting. There is no greater turn-off than to leave your friends and race home from college for a family foundation meeting, only to find that all the funds are already allocated by the senior generation. Too many rules and restrictions around grant-making can also alienate younger family members, especially if they had no voice in setting up those rules. Alternatively, think of subjects that will draw them in. For example, we have seen many families effectively include impact or sustainable investing in their philanthropic entities. These types of investing attract family members of all ages, but they may particularly appeal to young people who are seeking to change the world in a variety of ways at once. Finally, remember the long-term goal:

engaging the rising generation in the habit of giving. If you disagree with some of their priorities or choices, it may be politic to hold your tongue. Let them learn if a grant turns out to be disappointing or inefficient. They will learn much more effectively from experience than from being told so by their elders.

Magnificence

We have given a strong recommendation for family philanthropy because we believe it is or can be a deeply positive experience. Professional philanthropists like to describe themselves using words like "efficient," "effective," and "strategic." While family philanthropy can be all these things, too, we believe that it can be more. At its best, it captures the quality of magnificence.

Magnificence is a virtue described first by Aristotle, a virtue of spending large amounts of money. One of the curious things about magnificence is that it need not strictly be charitable. It can encompass charity, but it may also involve spending to get a return. In this sense, it can encompass what today is called socially responsible investing: investing to get a return both for yourself and for others.

The most important feature of magnificence is that it is fitting: the expenditure fits the person doing it, the person receiving it, and the occasion. A very beautiful toy may be a magnificent gift for a child, even if it does not cost a lot. A small charitable donation—or a small investment—that helps launch a new, ground-breaking institution could also be magnificent.

Aristotle also says that the magnificent expenditure evokes wonder. It causes others to look less at us—the spenders—and more at the result. And that result, he says, is "cosmic," literally, "an ordered whole." A magnificent expenditure brings people together. Maybe that is through setting up a school, or funding a factory, or hosting a splendid gala. By evoking our human response to beauty and order, magnificence inspires reflection and hope.

However, if these thoughts on magnificence sound like they are temptations to pride, here is one more point to consider: while charitable recipients need such things as food, clothing, and shelter, philanthropists need something, too: charitable recipients. Families do not meet in boardrooms for their own sake. Nor do they make site visits or read grant proposals or learn about organizational efficiencies for the fun of it. They do all these things for the sake of the health, education, and growth of their charitable recipients. The well-being of charitable recipients is the true end or goal of family philanthropy, as it is for philanthropy more generally.

Individual Flourishing

To accomplish great things, we must not only act, but also dream; not only plan, but also believe.

Anatole France

Many Blossoms

As we mentioned at the beginning of this book, one of our key principles is that families' true assets are the individuals who comprise them. A flourishing family is composed of flourishing individuals; family well-being rests on individual well-being.

Our focus throughout this book has been on activities that families can take together to encourage that true "wealth as well-being," especially amid great financial capital. These practices have ranged from certain types of giving, to self-exploration, to methods of communicating as spouses or grandparents, to practices specific to trusteeship, family meetings, or family philanthropy.

But all this activity presupposes the goal: individual flourishing. Flourishing is a highly personal topic. For example, at a family retreat we led, the group discussed, "What is flourishing?" They came up with a variety of answers, such as the following:

- Thriving
- Growing
- Self-sustaining

175

- Beautiful
- Harmonious
- Dramatic and alive
- Abundant
- Conscious
- Full of life
- Many blossoms

While flourishing is a somewhat subjective matter, we do not want to end without saying something about what it looks like, at least to us.

The Five Ls

We have found that the simplest way to describe individual flourishing, and one that has resonated with hundreds of families and audiences, is an adaptation that we have made of the account of flourishing offered by Dr. Barrie Greiff in his book *Legacy* (New York: Random House, 2000). Dr. Greiff is a psychiatrist who has worked with hundreds of patients. From his work, we have derived what we call the Five Ls: learn, labor, love, laugh, and leave (or let go).

1. *Learn*: A fundamental part of individual flourishing is learning. As the Greek poet and politician Solon wrote in advanced old age, "I grow older always learning." Or as Aristotle wrote in the opening line of his *Metaphysics*, "All human beings desire to know." Not everybody loves education—and we have been careful in this book not to urge "family wealth education programs." Yet everyone loves to learn. This desire is core to being human; its activation is part of our human flourishing.

2. *Labor*: We have already written about the centrality of work to a sense of identity, purpose, and meaning. This labor does not need to be compensated financially. What is crucial is that we feel that it engages our true strengths for the benefit of others.

3. *Love*: Even in a world suffused by commercial relationships, in which everyone supposedly looks out only for himself, love still lies at the center of human happiness and misery. Much of this book has been about how to maintain the humanity of human relationships even amid great financial and legal structures.

4. *Laugh*: Money is supposed to be a serious matter. That appearance is one way it maintains its power. Laughter is a release from the shoulds and woulds of life. When we are tempted to be pompous, it reminds us of our foolishness. It is the great equalizer in communities, including families. It is also a balm to pain. It is no wonder that children's hospitals around the world bring clowns in to bring their patients some joy.

5. *Leave* (or *let go*): Many spiritual traditions teach that the great source of suffering in human life is attachment, above all the demand that things be (or remain) the way I want them to be (or remain). Letting go of such attachment is the path to relieving suffering and allowing yourself to flourish in the moment, as things are.

As you read this list of the Five Ls, think about yourself. Which of these five do you find it easiest to actualize in your life? Which the hardest? What steps can you take now to begin to live all five? How can others around you, including in your family, help you in this pursuit of individual flourishing? How can you help them?

The Four Cs

The Five Ls can help you picture a sort of portfolio of flourishing: where you are strong and where you are underperforming. They provide a sense of the goal.

To help get to that goal, we use another tool, which we call the Four Cs. We introduced these Four Cs in Chapter 4, in relation to the rising generation's task of rising, but they apply to anyone at any stage of life.

The Four Cs come from studies of resilience, that is, the ability to bounce from whatever the world throws your way. Resilience is the key factor in determining whether we will succeed or suffer in any given endeavor.

Resilience involves a number of components, including having a good physical and mental state and a strong, supportive social network. But perhaps the most important component in resilience is your mental attitude. The attitude we have in mind here is what psychologists call self-efficacy; simply, the belief that you can "do it"; you can meet whatever life sends your way with grace and integrity.

The Four Cs contribute to self-efficacy. They are control, commitment, challenge, and community. They are opposed to powerlessness, alienation, threat, and isolation (see Figure C.1).

C.1   The Four Cs.

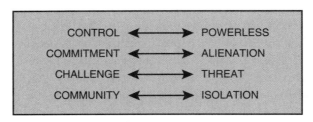

To use the Four Cs as a tool, think about the space between each C and its opposite as a spectrum. Then think about particularly important situations or circumstances in your life, such as a job or relationship or important choice. Where are you in each spectrum? Are you feeling in control or powerless? Do you feel committed or alienated? Do you feel challenged or threatened? Do you feel that you have a community behind you or are you feeling isolated?

The Four Cs are a powerful tool for flourishing generally. They have special relevance when great financial capital is part of your life. For great financial capital can have the effect of pushing people toward the opposite of each C. If you have made a great fortune, you can feel powerless to keep it—or make sure it does not hurt those you love. If you inherited a great fortune, you may feel disempowered by trusts or other instruments. Great wealth-creators or heirs can feel committed in some ways (such as in philanthropy) but alienated from many other pursuits enjoyed by their peers. Wealth-holders may also feel threatened by others, whom they perceive as targeting them for their riches. Finally, there is no doubt that great financial capital can leave its holders feeling isolated from the rest of society—and even from their spouses and children.

Again, with the Five Ls in mind as a goal, apply the Four Cs to these goals. Do you feel in control, committed, challenged, and in community when it comes to learning, laboring, loving, laughing, and leaving? None of us will feel that we are flourishing in all these ways at the same time. But intentionality can bring us closer, enriching our lives and the lives of those around us.

Three Little Words

We close with three words that, appropriately, came to us as a sort of inspiration when speaking to a roomful of family members. The three of us were on a panel together. The moderator asked us each to share an insight with the crowd. Jay and then Keith took up about 39 of the 40 minutes allocated to all three of us to answer. The host then turned to Susan and asked for her input. In the minute left to her she replied, "As I reflect on what Jay and Keith have shared with you, there are three words I would like to add to their comments. They are humility, empathy, and hope." We have no doubt that they were the best things that audience took away with them that day. We share them here with you:

1. *Humility*: The journey of complete family wealth is hard. As our opening quotation in the epigraph from Thales suggests, it is easy to tell others what to do. It is very hard to know your own heart and to pursue it bravely. These matters of family and money can be devilishly difficult to untangle with a clear mind and calm breast. Even after studying, practicing, and living these matters for decades, with clients and our own families, we often find ourselves at square one. It is truly a journey requiring a "beginner's mind."

2. *Empathy*: We have written about the importance of empathy in family relationships, of the ability to take yourself out of your own head and to put yourself into others' shoes. Here we would take one step further and stress the importance of empathizing with yourself. So often we are expected to have all the answers, or we expect ourselves always to do the right thing and make the right choices. The journey of family wealth and of life generally is one in which missteps likely outnumber those right choices. Self-compassion is a necessity.

3. *Hope*: One of the constants we have seen in the decades since the publication of *Family Wealth* is the public fascination with stories of wealthy families who have come to grief. However, in recent years we have also noticed more public attention to families who have done well and succeeded over generations, and we have seen more and more families willing to come together to talk about factors in their success. Much of our work is meant to highlight these possibilities. Family wealth need not be a tale of woe. Individuals do grow up happy and healthy. Families do stay together. It can be done.

As the time comes, now, to put back on your regalia and take up your scallop shell, the time to set out on—or continue—your own journey, do so with our thanks for the opportunity to share our gifts with you and with our hopes, as Cavafy wrote, that your journey "be long/full of adventures, full of knowledge."

Epilogue: The Future?

The exercise of writing this book and looking back at the last 50 years of our practice has also led us to consider what the world of family wealth might look like 50 or 100 years from now. These are our brief exploratory thoughts on this question. Like any predictions, they may be wide of the mark. We hope that they encourage you to fulfill your responsibility in the work of growing complete family wealth by thinking about what the far-off future looks like to you.

Evolutions in Human Development

Over the last generation, a whole new developmental stage has appeared, "emergent adulthood." It has had an immense impact on education, work, housing, marriage, and extended family structure. Misunderstanding this new stage has had huge effects on giving within families and the transitions of family enterprises. To cite just one example that we have seen play out lately: appeals to "stewardship" as a value may have little resonance for emergent adults, leading to fractures and recriminations amid family leadership.

At the same time, more and more family members are finding themselves in an extended stage of late-middle age, facing the dilemma of generativity or stagnation. How they face this dilemma will have an extraordinary impact on philanthropy, economic growth, and family dynamics.

One area of possibility we see ahead is a growing seriousness about elder-ship within families: elders, not just seniors. The path to eldership is clearer among some Eastern societies. It remains a question whether the West can learn the importance of elders and adapt their role to our changing families. The well-being or misery of millions of aging family members—and their families—hangs in the balance.

Changes in Family Structure

It is clear today that forms of family are emerging that are far removed from the "norm" of family as a married man and woman and their biological children. Such changes will likely accelerate.

One change is the "inversion" of family membership that is taking place due to the deep reduction in children born in the developed world and in China over the last 50 to 100 years, ever since the move away from an agriculture-based economy.

The traditional growth in the number of family members led to a situation in which families' assets were overwhelmed by their numbers. Now, and likely for at least the next 50 years, if not permanently, many families will have one child or two, and many of those children will elect to have no children. This is already the state of reality in Japan, China, western Europe, Russia, the United States, and in most other developed countries.

This change brings great freedom to adults, especially women, who can pursue other endeavors besides child-rearing. It may lead to increased philanthropy, as people have fewer heirs. But it could also cause families and societies at large to suffer a huge and perhaps irreversible reduction in their qualitative capital. It puts a terrific strain on the social compact between the young and the old. It makes even more important the efforts to maximize the qualitative capitals.

A related change in family structure is the likely redistribution of property by gender, away from men and toward women, as women continue to live longer than men and now also inherit more and create much more wealth than they did in the past. No one knows yet what effect this historic change— the "fiscal differences" we described in Chapter 7—will have on men and the families and societies they are part of.

New Understandings of Family Wealth

Though the threat of government sequestration of private wealth still arises at times and makes the use of international trust structures attractive, it is much less prevalent than in the past. With the liberalization of tax laws, trusts are coming to be seen less about reducing taxes and more about creating positive human outcomes for families. If the new understanding of trusts as human relationships changes the number of beneficiaries who feel their trusts are burdens from 80 percent to only 50 percent, a great good will emerge in the world.

A related development that we see just starting to gain strength in family offices around the world is serious attention to *learning* (not just *education*) as a family activity. Many investors today would not invest in a company that does not have a Chief Learning Officer, or a similar officer tasked with continually growing the company's intellectual capital. Likewise, families are coming to see that if they are going to compete for resources with these companies, they must take learning just as seriously. Over time, we expect the "Chief Learning Officer"—whether outsourced or in-house—to be a regular feature of family systems, similar to a trustee or chief investment officer. This function will help ensure that all family members learn to make better decisions together and develop their capacities to the fullest. This will be a great development for individual and family flourishing.

China

For the last 200 years or so, accounts of the future have always had to take account of China. The same is the case in this field: it is hard to imagine China not playing a prominent role in the future of family wealth. We have already referred to the changes in family structure and governance occasioned by the former "one-child" policy. This policy itself stands against the backdrop of the Cultural Revolution's murder of wealth-holders, breaking up of families, and burning of books that spoke to family harmony. These are the conditions under which the immense growth of private wealth in the 1980s and, in a second wave, in the late 1990s and early 2000s, has emerged. As a result, wealth is set to transfer in China with an almost complete lack of preparation.

In addition, informal surveys suggest that many wealth-holders want to emigrate and are struggling with a clash between uneducated parents and grandparents versus Western-educated children and grandchildren.

China has a history of adapting Western ideas and technology for itself. Family wealth—the principles and practices of its preservation and growth—may be one of the most promising of such ideas for the future of China and, as a result, for the larger world that it undoubtedly will affect. Similarly, there may be much that Western families—who traditionally have looked to Europe to learn about the long-term consequences of family financial wealth—can learn from China.

Appendix One: Fiduciary Course Curriculum

Introduction

This eight-session course is designed for future family leaders. The overall goals of the course are the following:

1. Engage future family leaders in active learning and in applying their learning to practice.
2. Ground future family leaders in knowledge of the basics of trusts and related fiduciary roles and responsibilities.
3. Continue to strengthen relationships between future family leaders with each other and with the trustees.
4. Prepare future family leaders to make informed choices about accepting fiduciary roles in the future.

Each session in the program will run for 90 minutes and include opportunities for instruction, self-reflection, and active discussion.

Overview of Sessions

Session One: The Fiduciary Mindset

This session will build familiarity with the fiduciary mindset. It will define what a fiduciary is and how trustees differ from other types of fiduciaries. It will then outline the five key principles to the fiduciary mindset: Do no harm, Fidelity, Regency, Discernment, and Courage. Participants will have a chance to discuss their hopes and concerns about possibly serving as fiduciaries.

Session Two: Trust Basics

This session will educate participants in the legal requirements for a trust; the types, rights, and responsibilities of beneficiaries; and the types, duties, and powers of trustees. Participants will have an opportunity to discuss how they would define a great beneficiary and how they would define a great trustee.

Session Three: Risk Management

This session will introduce participants to two key aspects of trust risk management: effective communication between trustees and beneficiaries, and effective transition planning. Participants will have a chance to discuss what sort of "contract" they think contributes to a healthy beneficiary-trustee relationship.

Session Four: The Trust Agreement and Trust Principles

This session will engage participants, through a "treasure hunt," in understanding important features of their trusts. It will also offer a brief review of the grantor's intent and wishes around the trusts. Participants will be encouraged to discuss what in these intentions they find helpful or challenging.

Session Five: Distributions

This session will review the basics of distributions and educate participants in the process of evaluating a distribution request. It will introduce the distinction of a prevention-focus versus a promotion-focus mindset and the "model for a humane trustscape" as enhancements to the distribution evaluation process. Participants will have an opportunity to discuss these ideas and their application to the complexity of evaluating distribution requests from family members.

Session Six: Trusts and the Enterprise

This session will locate family trusts within the larger context of the family enterprise, especially as concerns the activity of investing within trusts and the governance of trusts vis-à-vis other enterprise governance bodies. Participants will be encouraged to discuss ways to capitalize on opportunities and address challenges that they see within the current enterprise.

Session Seven: Special Considerations

This session will take up three special considerations: (1) the treatment of trusts in the context of marriage; (2) planning for beneficiaries with mental or emotional special needs or addiction; and (3) building processes of accountability and enhancement of the trust system.

Session Eight: Bringing It All Together

The goals of this session are to review the course learning and to engage participants in a discussion of what action items they would like to take or to propose to the proper authorities to implement their learning.

Fiduciary Curriculum Outline

Session One: The Fiduciary Mindset (90 minutes)

I. What is a fiduciary? (10 minutes)
 a. Different types.
 b. Fiduciary principle: acting on behalf of someone for the benefit of someone else.
 c. Problem: why is a trustee important? Alternatives . . .
  i. Technical application of grantor's wishes.
  ii. Technical processing of beneficiary's wishes.
 d. Principle of common good: grantor's vision infusing and infused by hopes/needs of community of beneficiaries.
 e. Role for trustees: community of interpretation—of the grantor's wishes and of the beneficiaries' dreams.
II. Principles of the Fiduciary Mindset (50 minutes)
 a. Differences among outcomes, process, principles, habits, and intention/mindset.
 b. First, Do No Harm.
  i. Danger of focusing on narrowly quantitative goals.
  ii. Define goals qualitatively.
  iii. Illustration: Family Balance Sheet's Five Qualitative Capitals: human, financial-educational, relationship, social, and legacy capitals.

   c. Fidelity
      i. Faithful not simply to document, grantor, or beneficiary.
      ii. Ultimately, faithful to keeping alive the spirit of the gift.
      iii. Illustration: gifts with spirit versus transfers.
   d. Regency
      i. Danger of paternalism, leading to beneficiary passivity.
      ii. Ultimate aim is beneficiary individuation.
      iii. Illustration: "ladder of giving": with more restrictive giving at bottom and "partnership" at top.
   e. Discernment
      i. Centrality to trust functions, especially distributive function.
      ii. Experience practicing discernment in "nub" scenarios.
      iii. Importance of fostering discernment in beneficiaries.
      iv. Illustration: discerning beneficiary needs via the developmental approach.
   f. Courage
      i. To acknowledge your own limitations and seek advice.
      ii. To stand firm even when it angers beneficiaries or grantor.
      iii. To plan for the system's successful transition to a new generation.
      iv. Illustration: moving trust system from grantor-centered to beneficiary-centered.
III. Self-reflection and discussion (25 minutes)
   a. What concerns do I have about serving as a fiduciary?
   b. What hopes do I have for serving as a fiduciary?
   c. Discussion of concerns, hopes, and questions about the fiduciary mindset.
IV. Concluding self-reflection (5 minutes)
   a. What attracts me most about the fiduciary mindset?
   b. What actions can I take to further develop that mindset?

Session Two: Trust Basics (90 minutes)

   I. Initial exercise (5 minutes)
   a. What's my narrative regarding trusts?
   II. What makes a trust (5 minutes)
   a. Legal requirements (intent, lawful purpose, property, beneficiary).
   b. Exercise: What's missing from this list? *Who's* missing?
   III. Trustscapes (10 minutes)
   a. Definition of a trustscape.
   b. Exercise: Drawing and comparing your trustscapes.

IV. Beneficiary basics (20 minutes)
  a. What's a beneficiary?
  b. Who decides who is a beneficiary?
  c. Types of beneficiaries (current, contingent, remainder).
  d. Beneficiary rights (enumerated and legal).
  e. Beneficiary responsibilities (respond, cooperate, communicate).
V. Trustee basics (20 minutes)
  a. What's a trustee? (Versus other fiduciaries?)
  b. Who decides who is a trustee?
  c. Types of trustees (individual [family member versus professional] and institutional).
  d. What trustees must do (duties).
    i. The big three: loyalty, impartiality, prudence.
    ii. Others.
  e. What trustees may do (powers).
VI. Self-reflection and discussion (30 minutes)
  a. How would I define a great beneficiary?
  b. How would I define a great trustee?
  c. Combine results to come up with shared descriptions.

Session Three: Risk Management (90 minutes)

I. Initial self-reflection (5 minutes)
  a. What do I see as the greatest risk in our trustscape, and how would I recommend managing that risk?
II. Effective communication as risk management (30 minutes)
  a. Exercise: seeing the world through the eyes of (i) the trustee and (ii) the beneficiary—comparing these perspectives.
  b. Evaluating relationships.
    i. Signs of positive beneficiary-trustee relationship.
    ii. Signs of a relationship in need of attention.
  c. Enhancing relationships.
    i. Cognitive-behavioral model.
    ii. The "Three-step process."
  d. Managing conflict.
    i. Assessing parties.
    ii. Assessing the system.
    iii. Identifying motivations for change.
    iv. Avenues for resolution.

   e. Managing litigation risk.
     i. Honest assessment of situation.
     ii. Annual process audit.
     iii. Judicious documentation procedures.
     iv. Importance of competent, timely counsel.
 III. Discussion (20 minutes)
   a. What sort of "contract" do I think would contribute to a healthy beneficiary-trustee relationship? (E.g., rules of engagement, expectations, accountability . . .)
 IV. Effective transition planning as part of risk management (30 minutes)
   a. Beneficiary powers of appointment.
   b. Trustee removal and appointment.
   c. Choosing a wise trustee.
     i. Pros and cons of different types of trustee (oneself, family member, professional, institution).
     ii. Delegation and direction.
     iii. Role of trust adviser.
     iv. Role of trust protector.
 V. Concluding self-reflection (5 minutes)
   a. What do I most want to hold onto from this session?
   b. What action do I want to take, based on this session?

Session Four: The Trust Agreement and Trust Principles (90 minutes)

 I. Trust Agreement Treasure Hunt (30 minutes)
   a. Basic questions.
     i. Who created the trust?
     ii. What is its discernible purpose?
     iii. When did it take effect?
     iv. Who is the trustee?
     v. Who is entitled to receive distributions now?
     vi. Who is entitled to receive distributions later? When?
   b. Questions about the trustee(s).
     i. What specific powers does the trustee have?
     ii. Who is the successor trustee?
     iii. Can the beneficiary remove and replace the trustee? If so, what are the conditions for that process?

　　c. Questions about trust distributions.
　　　　i. Are any distributions automatic or scheduled?
　　　　ii. What purposes are set to guide discretionary distributions?
　　d. Questions on the trust's termination.
　　　　i. Does my trust come to an end? When?
　　　　ii. What happens to the trust property when this trust ends?
　　　　iii. Does someone have the right to determine who receives trust property when the trust ends? Who and how?
II. The Grantor's Intent and Wishes: Brief Review (30 minutes)
　　a. Intentions drawn from Letter of Intent.
　　b. Any other expressions of Grantor's wishes.
III. Discussion (25 minutes)
　　a. What results in the treasure hunt surprised me? Confused me? What questions remain?
　　b. Which wishes from the Grantor have contributed most to my living well?
　　c. Which wishes or intentions do I find most challenging?
　　d. If I were a trustee, how would I think through handling an intention that I found difficult or even counterproductive to apply in a given case?
IV. Concluding self-reflection (5 minutes)
　　a. What do I most want to hold onto from this session?
　　b. What do I want to learn more about, either regarding the trust agreement or the Grantor's intentions and wishes?

Session Five: Distributions (90 minutes)

I. Distribution basics (10 minutes)
　　a. Three main functions of a trust (administration, investment, distributions).
　　b. Types of distribution: mandatory and discretionary.
　　c. Types of discretionary distributions.
　　　　i. HEMS (Health, Education, Maintenance, and Support).
　　　　ii. Absolute discretion.
　　　　iii. Exercise: defining possible distributions as HEMS or not.
　　d. Distinguishing trust distributions from parental gifts.
II. Evaluating a distribution request (30 minutes)
　　a. Importance of documentation.
　　b. Description of request process.

        i. Written request.

       ii. Required supporting documentation.

      iii. Timeline.

   c. Analysis of request.

        i. Distribution standards.

       ii. Beneficiary purpose.

      iii. Grantor principles.

      iv. Trustee duties (loyalty, impartiality, prudence).

       v. Other options.

      vi. Other resources.

     vii. Other considerations.

   d. Importance of mindset: prevention-focus versus promotion-focus.

        i. Context (tax return versus party planning).

       ii. Types of responses to requests.

      iii. Focusing on strengths versus problems.

      iv. Exercise: use a few actual distribution requests (anonymized) to practice recognizing and moving between prevention-focus versus promotion-focus mindset.

III. "Model for a Humane Trustscape" as applied to distributions (10 minutes)

   a. Distribution committee or distribution adviser.

   b. "Beneficiary Advisory Board": input from beneficiary mentors.

   c. "Trust Champion": use of trust protector or similar non-fiduciary elder to mediate beneficiary-trustee disagreements.

IV. Discussion (30 minutes)

   a. What challenges do I see to evaluating distribution requests from my own family members?

   b. How would I address those challenges?

V. Concluding self-reflection (10 minutes)

   a. How has my learning in this session changed my "narrative" regarding trust distributions?

   b. What action, if any, would I like to take based on that learning?

Session Six: Trusts and the Enterprise (90 minutes)

I. Definition of the enterprise (20 minutes)

   a. Family Enterprise Board or Family Council.

   b. Family trusts.

   c. Closely-held business interests.

    d. Philanthropic entities.

    e. Other?

II. Investing in the context of trusts (20 minutes)

    a. General considerations ("Prudent Man" versus Modern Portfolio Theory).

    b. "Direction" of trustees regarding investments.

    c. Investor allocation.

    d. Treatment of closely-held business interests.

III. Governance (20 minutes)

    a. Promoting communication within the enterprise.

    b. Identifying proper level of decision-making.

    c. Resolving conflicts between enterprise entities.

IV. Discussion (25 minutes)

    a. What challenges do I see to managing trusts well within our family enterprise?

    b. How would I address those challenges?

V. Closing self-reflection (5 minutes)

    a. What steps would I like to take to understand and contribute to the enhancement of our family enterprise?

Session Seven: Special Considerations

I. Initial self-reflection (5 minutes)

    a. What is a gift I have received that has truly made a positive impact in my life?

II. Trusts and marriage (25 minutes)

    a. Prenups and trusts.

        i. Legal process and considerations.

        ii. Prenups as a family "norm."

        iii. Communicating about prenups.

        iv. Exercise: what has worked or not worked in talking about prenups with (a) your parents and (b) your prospective spouse?

    b. Treatment of spouses based on the Grantor's intentions and wishes.

    c. Using the "Three-Step Process" for talking with your spouse about your trust.

III. Trusts and special needs (25 minutes)

    a. Planning for beneficiaries with mental impairment.

    b. Planning for beneficiaries with emotional challenges.

    c. Planning for beneficiaries with addiction.

IV. Accountability and enhancement (30 minutes)
   a. Accountability of trustees and of beneficiaries.
      i. Standards of evaluation?
      ii. Means of evaluation?
      iii. By whom?
      iv. To whom?
      v. Regularity?
      vi. Consequences?
   b. Enhancement of the trustscape: "Trust Champion"/protector to . . .
      i. Convene regular review.
      ii. Promote innovation through forecasting and learning.
V. Concluding self-reflection (5 minutes)
   a. What do I want most to hold onto from this session?
   b. What action would I like to take, based on my learning?

Session Eight: Bringing It All Together (90 minutes)

I. Initial self-reflection (5 minutes)
   a. What has stayed most with me from the prior sessions?
   b. What do I feel was missing?
II. Review of prior sessions (20 minutes)
III. Discussion of possible action items (60 minutes)
   a. What specific proposals or recommendations would members of this group like to make?
   b. Who has the authority to decide on specific proposals or recommendations? For example, individuals, the trustees, the Brothers Council, family as a whole?
IV. Concluding self-reflection (5 minutes)
   a. What in this learning process am I most grateful for?
   b. What action items am I most excited to engage in?

Appendix Two: Key Practices for Families During Challenging Times

Introduction

The COVID-19 pandemic, and the effects that it has had on society, markets, families, and individuals, have subjected us all to a storm of different emotions and conflicting information. In this Appendix, we have collected in one place key practices that can help you and your family navigate similarly trying times. While some of these practices are most relevant to families with wealth, many of them apply with or without wealth. We focus on practices for families, but since healthy families are made of up healthy individuals, we will end with several key practices for individuals to navigate challenging times.

Key Practices for Families

Key Practice 1: Being Aware of Emotional "Hot Buttons"

We all have "emotional hot buttons," and those hot buttons are more sensitive under stress. To manage interactions among family members that intensify when emotional hot buttons are pushed, there are several things you can do:

- If you feel things are getting heated, give yourself a "pause." An easy way to do this is to count to 10 before replying to something that's been said.
- During the pause, try to recognize what part you are playing in the exchange. Emotional interactions are never one-sided.
- Be aware of yourself and what you're feeling. Is it Frustration? Fear? Sadness? Worry? Anger?

- Assume that the person you're talking with has good intent toward you. This assumption will take a lot of the "heat" out of the exchange.
- Cultivate your own good intent toward others. At a time when most people feel some fear and sadness, kindness and empathy might be among our most important assets.

Key Practice 2: Recognizing Different Communication Styles

We all have our preferred styles of communicating with others, and stress tends to make those styles more rigid. Recognizing our own and others' styles can help us communicate more effectively, especially during difficult times. The following chart summaries four main communication styles:

Style	Characteristics	Under stress
Drivers	Action-oriented with focus on making decisions	May become more controlling and impatient
Analytics	Logic- and process-oriented	May withdraw, become more hesitant and risk-averse
Expressives	Energetic, creative, communicative	May become overly emotional and verbally aggressive
Amiables	Steady, agreeable, team-players	May become acquiescent and eager to please

Key Practice 3: Balancing Togetherness and Separateness

In normal times, financial wealth has a "centripetal" effect, that is, it often leads to more family togetherness than if it did not exist. Family members may share vacation homes, trips, vehicles, and holidays, as well as investment accounts or trusts. As a result, families with wealth should regularly discuss their desired balance of togetherness and separateness. Some family members may want more togetherness, while others would prefer more separation. The important things are to listen to, understand each other, and make appropriate accommodations.

In challenging times, when due to "shelter-in-place" orders or travel restrictions, many of us may be seeing more of our families than we usually do, we also recommend thoughtfully talking over these points:

- If you're living together, what "ground rules" would make the situation more enjoyable (e.g., rules about noise, vehicle use, visitors, ways of speaking and acting with respect toward each other)?

- How will common spaces (e.g., kitchens, living rooms, game rooms) be used and maintained?
- How can family members who are working remotely maintain quiet, distraction-free workspace?
- At what times or under what conditions are each other's rooms or houses "open for visits"?
- What signals can family members use to indicate to each other that they need some space, physical or psychological?

Key Practice 4: Talking about Serious Matters

Empathic communication is crucial for talking about serious matters that might have felt low-priority or hard to discuss before the current crisis. For example, access to food, needed medications, safe clinical environments, as well as personal security. As part of responsible planning, many families have been reviewing their emergency plans. Where would a family member go if he or she became ill? Who are family members' medical proxies? Who will watch children if parents are sick or need to quarantine themselves?

Key Practice 5: Reviewing Governance

Governance means deciding how you make decisions. Some families govern themselves informally. Others have highly developed governance structures, such as boards or Family Councils. Thinking about governance can feel low-importance right now. But all these activities—from emergency-preparedness, to ground rules for togetherness, to something as simple as organizing a call—involve governance, because they all involve decision-making.

Take a moment to ask yourself: "What specific decisions does my family face in the current crisis? How can we best make those decisions?"

Times of crisis lead many families to look hard at their governance. Some realize that it is time to advance long-standing plans to devolve decision-making from family elders to the rising generation, perhaps with subset of members as an executive team. Other families recognize the true value of involving non-family experts, such as trustees or other advisers, in their deliberations and decision-making. Many families have recognized that effective decision-making also requires more regular communication.

Governance can and should adapt to circumstances. The key is that your family feel able to discuss and make those changes openly and thoughtfully.

Key Practice 6: Making the Most of Your Advisers/Family Office

One of the hardest aspects of a crisis can be physical isolation, combined with a news cycle that never sleeps and often seems very alarming. During such times, we recommend that family members communicate more with their advisers or family office staff rather than less. This is an opportunity to remind yourself of your financial or legal plans; to review how those plans are performing; and to reaffirm or reevaluate your decisions. It can also be an opportunity to learn, from your advisers, how other families are addressing these challenging times or to share, via a family office, how different households in your family are doing. If you have questions for your advisers, ask them. Seek more frequent, even if shorter, interactions to stay in touch.

Key Practices for Individuals

As we mentioned at the beginning of this Appendix, healthy families are made up of healthy individuals. Let's take a moment to review key practices for individuals to navigate challenging times. You may want to use this opportunity to step back for a moment and reflect on which of these practices you are using now, and which you would like to integrate into your daily life.

Key Practice 7: Caring for Yourself Physically

Nutrition

Nutrition is fundamental to physical care. Stress can cause us to eat too much, too little, or not well. Listen to your body and observe your choices.

Exercise

Besides promoting health, exercise clears the mind and lifts the spirits. Exercise has often been described as nature's anti-anxiety and anti-depressant medication. It can be a challenge to exercise if you do not have access to your usual gym or pool or the like. However, it is important to get outside, take walks, run, or bike.

Relaxation

Relaxing may involve turning off the news, setting aside email or texts, and not focusing on the financial markets. Perhaps set aside time each day when you can catch up on the latest news or necessary communications. You may also want to try practices such as meditation or yoga or simple, relaxing reading.

Key Practice 8: Fostering Quality Social Connections

Quality relationships are with people who help us focus forward, on what we can do; who help us problem solve; and who affirm us. Research shows us that quality relationships are critical to helping people get through difficult times. Which quality social connections do you want to foster?

Key Practice 9: Mind Training—Making Your Mind Work for You

In a crisis, we need to develop the ability to be our own psychologists, as it were, and to diagnose how our heads are doing. Ask yourself: Am I having a hard time making decisions and focusing? Do I find myself feeling anxious, scared, down, or hopeless? Is my sleep disrupted? Noticing these things is the beginning of taking your own mental "temperature."

After you've assessed how you're feeling, stop and notice what you are saying to yourself about the situation. Try to look through the emotions to the statements that your inner voice repeats. Once you've listened to what you're telling yourself, then ask this simple question, "Is what I am saying to myself useful?"

This process of reflection can help remind you of experiences that provide ground for realistic hope. Reflect on how you managed difficult times in the past. Whatever the nature of past crises (medical, familial, financial, etc.), ask yourself, "What skills, knowledge, and choices allowed me to find my way through?"

Conclusion

In this Appendix we have shared nine key practices for navigating challenging times, as families and as individuals:

1. Being aware of "emotional hot buttons."
2. Recognizing different communication styles.
3. Balancing togetherness and separateness.
4. Talking about serious matters.
5. Reviewing governance.
6. Making the most of your advisers/family office.

7. Caring for yourself physically.
8. Fostering quality social connections.
9. Mind training—making your mind work for you.

We will end with one more:

Key Practice 10: Expressing gratitude

Whether it is at a family meeting or a family dinner (in-person or virtual), at the end of the gathering, consider asking encourage each participant to share something he or she is grateful for. In times when we all feel at risk, when so much has been taken away, remind yourself, through gratitude, of what you still have and what matters most.

About the Authors

James E. Hughes Jr., Esq.

A retired attorney and resident of Aspen, Colorado, Jay is the author or coauthor of *Family Wealth: Keeping It in the Family*; *Family: The Compact Among Generations*; *Cycle of the Gift: Family Wealth & Wisdom*; *Voice of the Rising Generation: Family Wealth & Wisdom*; *Family Trusts: A Guide for Beneficiaries, Trustees, Trust Protectors, and Trust Creators*; and numerous articles on family governance and wealth preservation.

Jay is the founder of a law partnership in New York City and has spoken at numerous international and domestic symposia on avoiding the loss of family wealth described in the "shirtsleeves-to-shirtsleeves in three generations" proverb and on growing families' qualitative capital.

Jay is a member of various philanthropic boards and a member of the editorial boards of various professional journals. He is a graduate of the Far Brook School, which teaches through the arts; The Pingry School; Princeton University; and the Columbia School of Law.

Dr. Susan E. Massenzio

Susan is a psychologist who sees wisdom as core to counsel. She is the cofounder and copresident of Wise Counsel Research, a think tank and consultancy. She is coauthor of *Cycle of the Gift* and *Voice of the Rising Generation*.

Susan has extensive experience consulting to senior executives, leadership teams of global financial services companies, and heads of family businesses. She helps firms develop high-potential executives, plan leadership succession, and integrate key leaders into new roles. She helps family leaders make a positive impact through enhanced communication, decision-making, cultivation of the next generation, and philanthropy.

Susan served for many years as the senior psychologist for John Hancock Financial Services, a senior vice president at Wells Fargo, and professor and program director at Northeastern University.

Susan holds a PhD in psychology from Northwestern University and a BA in sociology and education from Simmons College.

Susan can be reached at susan@wisecounselresearch.com.

Dr. Keith Whitaker

Keith is an educator and cofounder and copresident of Wise Counsel Research, a think tank and consultancy. He is coauthor of *Wealth and the Will of God*; *Cycle of the Gift*; *Voice of the Rising Generation*; *Family Trusts*, and *Wealth of Wisdom: The Top 50 Questions Wealthy Families Ask*. He is also the author of numerous books and articles in the field of classical political philosophy.

Keith has many years' experience consulting with advisers to and leaders of enterprising families. He helps families plan succession, develop next-generation talent, and communicate around estate planning. With a background in education and philanthropy, he enables family leaders to better understand their values and goals as well as how to have a positive impact on the world around them.

Keith served as a managing director at Wells Fargo, where he founded the innovative Family Dynamics Practice. He has also served as a researcher at the Center on Wealth and Philanthropy, and as an adjunct assistant professor of philosophy at Boston College.

Keith is the chairman of the board of the National Association of Scholars. He holds a PhD in social thought from the University of Chicago and a BA and an MA in classics and philosophy from Boston University.

Keith can be reached at keith@wisecounselresearch.com.

Index